Cultural Life
in the Federal Republic of Germany

A survey

Inter Nationes   Bonn

Introduction

Cultural life in the Federal Republic of Germany, marked by a great diversity of forms of expression and inherent natural contradictions, has its roots in centuries of history and German traditions. Developments in the cultural sphere in this country are also a part of European culture, even where political frontiers make divisions apparent.

Our country's diversity of cultural existence derives its strength from a political constitution that guarantees freedom of art and scholarship, of research and teaching. This constitution also provides a foundation for the fact that responsibility for culture lies with the individual *Laender* to the extent that the state can be involved in such activities at all. Apart from looking after cultural policy directed abroad, the federal authorities have few powers, limited to drawing up general guidelines which never encroach on the rights of the *Laender*. The resultant polycentrism within cultural life in the Federal Republic of Germany is a continuation of German traditions going back for centuries. From the Middle Ages onwards, a many-sided cultural existence developed in provincial capitals large and small, in principalities temporal and ecclesiastical, without being focused on a single metropolis. That only changed with establishment of the Reich in 1871, but the member states of the German Reich were, however, still left a large degree of independence in the cultural sphere.

Cover page 1:
Modern technology in the theatre. Laser beams were used in a Munich production of Mozart's "Magic Flute" for presentation of the realm of the Queen of the Night.

Opposite the title page: David Bennent as the main character in the film of "The Tin Drum". See also page 187.

Opposite: The "Street Art" activities organised by many local authorities promote discussion of contemporary art – in this case Niki de Saint Phalle's "Nana" at Hanover in 1974.

The regulation and strangulation of almost all cultural activities during the National Socialist rule of despotism and violence in the years from 1933 to 1945 inflicted severe wounds on cultural development in Germany during that period, and also caused lasting damage to the country's cultural reputation abroad. The defeat of the Third Reich during the Second World War (1939–1945) was accompanied by the breakdown of extensive areas of German cultural life. The intellectual and artistic forces that rose again immediately after 1945 quickly brought about a fresh start though. Within the area of the Federal Republic of Germany, set up in 1949, there was rapid political, social, economic, scientific, and cultural regeneration that took effect in the early 1950s, allowing the people of this country to gain fresh confidence in themselves and in their creative powers and capabilities.

Theatre productions and concert performances which soon attracted attention again and sometimes remain in the memory up to the present day, museums that gained a high reputation and exhibitions that aroused international interest, the new impact of German literature, and the continuing achievement of German architects and conservors of historic monuments – all that testifies to the vitality of cultural life in this country. Mention should also be made in this connection of the rapidly established reputation enjoyed by radio and television in the Federal Republic of Germany, and of the recently regained international standing of the German film.

This brochure aims at providing some idea of the diversity involved in selected spheres of cultural life. The descriptions are kept short so that the overall picture remains clear. No claim is made to completeness. The independent nature of these descriptions is also demonstrated by the fact that their authors have adhered to their individual views and evaluations. This brochure is not intended as replacement for a reference work. The intention is to stimulate the reader, to arouse his interest, and also to be a source of pleasure in this combination of information in words and pictures.

Stamps are sometimes referred to as "Post Office works of art". They also reflect cultural life in the Federal Republic of Germany.

DEUTSCHE BUNDESPOST
Alois Senefelder
1797
25
175 Jahre Flachdruckverfahren
1972

DEUTSCHE BUNDESPOST
WEIHNACHTSMARKE 1971
20 +10

15. Europäische Kunstausstellung
G.Grosz . 1970
70 DEUTSCHE BUNDESPOST BERLIN

DEUTSCHE BUNDESPOST
50
LANDSHUTER HOCHZEIT 1475

XX.
Internationale
Filmfestspiele
Berlin
30
DEUTSCHE BUNDESPOST
BERLIN
1970

20
DEUTSCHE BUNDESPOST BERLIN
LEUCHTTURM

DEUTSCHE BUNDESPOST
Hedda Gabler
50
LOUISE DUMONT
1862–1932
1976

FLUGHAFEN BERLIN-TEGEL
DEUTSCHE BUNDESPOST BERLIN
50
1974

LOVIS CORINTH 1858–1925
50
DEUTSCHE BUNDESPOST BERLIN
1975

1869/1969 HOCHSCHULE FÜR MUSIK
30
JOSEPH JOACHIM
DEUTSCHE BUNDESPOST BERLIN
1969

GEORG KOLBE 1877–1947
30
DEUTSCHE BUNDESPOST BERLIN
1977

DEUTSCHE BUNDESPOST
20
Mainz-Gutenberg-Museum

Contents

Literature   11

The visual arts   35

Museums and exhibitions   55

Theatre   73

Music   97

Arts and crafts   115

*Architecture and conservation of historic
monuments*   131

Design   157

Film and television   169

Customs and festivities   199

Encounter and exchange   215

Appendix

Supplementary Addresses   228

Register of names   238

Literature

No-one would assert today that the end of the war in 1945 marked a completely "fresh start" for German literature. There was no new beginning without reference to the past, either for the authors of "inner emigration" (Gottfried Benn, Werner Bergengruen, Hans Carossa, Friedrich Georg Jünger, Ernst Wiechert) or for those returning from exile whether in person or through their works (Bertolt Brecht, Hermann Broch, Alfred Döblin, Heinrich Mann, Thomas Mann, Stefan Zweig). Even for the younger authors of the "deforestation" (Wolfgang Weyrauch) fascist language and literature were the polemical negative to their poetics of a consciously impoverished language concentrating on the realistic detail. In the initial postwar years these three literatures existed alongside rather than together with one another.

Modern German postwar writing was shaped and determined by the "literature of the ruins". Drama (Wolfgang Borchert, "The Man Outside", 1947), prose (Heinrich Böll, "The Train Was on Time", 1949; "Traveller, if You Come to Spa", 1950; and Wolfdietrich Schnurre, "Die Rohrdommel ruft jeden Tag", 1950), and, above all, poetry were the poetic forms of a literature that sought to come to terms with both the reality of ruins and rubble, and the downfall of ideals and hopes. Mention should be made here of Weyrauch ("An die Wand geschrieben", 1950), Günter Eich ("Abgelegene Gehöfte", 1948, and

The German Book Trade's Peace Prize has been awarded annually since 1950. In 1979 the Prize went to violinist Yehudi Menuhin (above r.), and in 1980 to Ernesto Cardenal (below l.), the Nicaraguan Minister of Education and member of his country's Revolutionary Council. Yehudi Menuhin gave the prize money away for charitable purposes, and Ernesto Cardenal devoted his money to establishment of a children's library in Nicaragua. Rolf Keller, the chairman of the German Book Trade Association, is also to be seen in both photos, presenting the award in Frankfurt's Paulskirche.

"Untergrundbahn", 1949), Peter Huchel ("Gedichte", 1948), and Karl Krolow ("Gedichte", 1948, and "Heimsuchung", 1948), authors whose beginnings in nature poetry largely lay in the time of National Socialist rule.

The decisive points of crystallisation for postwar literature were the literary-cum-political magazines ("Aufbau", "Frankfurter Hefte", "Merkur", "Der Monat", "Ost und West", and "Der Ruf") and the "Gruppe 47" set up by Hans Werner Richter, which met at least once a year until 1967 for gatherings focusing around readings from unpublished works and presentation of the Group's coveted prize. Particularly during the 1950s when literature and politics were furthest apart, the "Gruppe 47" was both a literary clique and also articulated literature's political claims, gaining standing as a moral opposition through proclamations, manifestos, and open letters. At the same time it promoted the internationalisation of German postwar literature, a development that received visible expression with the award of the Nobel Prize to Heinrich Böll in 1972.

The literature of the Fifties, the years of political, economic, and social reconstruction, of rearmament, of joining NATO, and of the Economic Miracle, is characterised by on the one hand continuation of facing up to the implications of the legacy of fascism (including its literature), and on the other by the attempt to make a literary impact on the present day. Drama and theatre in the Federal Republic of that time did not get far with either. Foreign authors – T.S. Eliot, Thornton Wilder, Eugène Ionesco, Albert Camus, and Jean-Paul Sartre – predominated in the theatre repertoire, and serious German contemporary drama came from Switzerland (Friedrich Dürrenmatt, "The Visit", 1956, and "The Physicists", 1962, and Max Frisch, "Andorra", 1961). The novel devoted the most obvious attention to the dual task of dealing with the past and criticising the present. Reflection of the fascist past and the present-day of the Economic Miracle were particularly interwoven in the novels of Alfred Andersch ("Flight to Afar", 1957, and "The Redhead", 1960), Heinrich Böll "Adam, Where Art Thou?", 1951, "The Unguarded House", 1954, and "Billiards at Half Past Nine", 1959), and Günter Grass ("The Tin Drum", 1959). The styles of writing range from a socially critical realism to grotesquely satirical distortion. The poetry of the 1950s is marked by two tendencies. Gottfried Benn propagated a form of retreat from contemporary reality with his concept of "spirit as counter-fortune", and Paul Celan expressed the experiences of fascism in his hermetic poems ("Mohn und Gedächtnis", 1952, and "Sprachgitter", 1959), whereas the works of such people as Hans Magnus Enzensberger ("Verteidigung der Wölfe", 1957, and "Landessprache", 1960) presented poetic involvement with political issues. Günter Eich gave an important boost to the radio play of the time, particularly with his "Träume" (1951). He succeeded in utilising radio to establish a (nightmare-like) world through language, and thus became the establisher of a tradition for many authors such as Ingeborg Bachmann, Wolfgang Hildesheimer, and Walter Jens. The experimental radio play of the Sixties mainly aimed at breaking down conventional language patterns and forms of perception. The most important authors here, often exponents of "Concrete Poetry", were Jürgen Becker, Ludwig Harig, Helmut Heissenbüttel, Dieter Kühn, and Franz Mon.

The literature of the 1960s, the years of the declining Economic Miracle and the Grand Coalition, of the Vietnam war and the Extra-parliamentary Opposition, was marked in all its forms by far-reaching politisation, making literature functional. Literature was meant to serve the political struggle. The poetry of such writers as F.C. Delius ("Wir Unternehmer", 1966), Erich Fried ("und Vietnam und", 1966, and "Zeitfragen", 1968), and Yaak Karsunke ("reden und ausreden", 1969) was therefore as much concerned with the class struggle and exploitation, with the student rebellion and the Vietnam war, as were the political songs of Franz Josef Degenhardt, Hans Dieter Hüsch, and Dieter Süverkrüp. Drama in German took up this politisation, taking historical and contemporary subject-matter as its themes, often in the form of documentary theatre. Rolf Hochhuth dealt with Pope Pius XII's attitude to the murder of the Jews in "The Representative" (1963), and with the bombing of Dresden in "Soldiers" (1967). Heinar Kipphardt was concerned with the responsibility of the scientist for research findings in "In der Sache J. Robert Oppenheimer" (1964); Günter Grass with Brecht's role during the 17th of June 1953 uprising in "Die Plebejer proben den Aufstand" (1966), and with the student rebellion in "Uptight" (1969); Peter Weiss with the extermination of the Jews in "The Investigation" (1965), and with the USA's war in South-East Asia in "Vietnam Diskurs" (1968); and Hans Magnus Enzensberger with the Cuban revolution in "Das Verhör von Habana" (1970). Authors coming from the tradition of the socially critical popular play in dialect brought oppressive everyday reality onto the stage rather than the big political themes. The main characters in the plays of Martin Sperr ("Jagdszenen aus Niederbayern", 1966) and Franz Xaver Kroetz ("Wildwechsel", 1971, and "Stallerhof", 1972) often lead an outsider's existence in a village community, coming to grief because of the constriction and narrow-mindedness of their surroundings.

The novel as an extensive epic form may not have been directly suitable for political activism, but the important novelists of the Sixties were nevertheless political authors. Heinrich Böll ("The Clown", 1963, "The End of a Mission", 1966, and "Group Portrait with Lady", 1971), Günter Grass ("Dog Years", 1963, "Local Anaesthetic", 1969, and "From the Diary of a Snail", 1972), and Martin Walser embody the kind of writer for whom literature and politics, social experience and aesthetic shaping, belong closely together. These consistently realistic novels increasingly took as their theme contemporary conflicts and problems in the Federal Republic of Germany whereas Uwe Johnson has been concerned with the division of Germany ("Speculations about Jakob", 1959, "Third Book about Achim", 1961, "Two Views", 1965, and three volumes of "Jahrestage" since 1970). Political objectives are pursued with literary means by the authors in the Dortmund "Gruppe 61" (Max von der Grün, "Irrlicht und Feuer", 1963, and "Stellenweise Glatteis", 1973. Erika Runge, "Bottroper Protokolle", 1968. Günter Wallraff, "Wir brauchen dich", 1966, "13 unerwünschte Reportagen", 1969, and "Der Aufmacher", 1977.), and in the "Literature of the World of Work Group" set up in 1969 by the Dortmund association. Their programme emphasises literary concern with the world of industrial work and its social problems. Literature here is also intended to serve the formation of political consciousness among writers. This is literature by workers and literature for workers all in one. Authors who are less concerned with interpreting rather than (apparently) unemotionally describing social reality can be grouped under the label of "a literature of description". The main writers here are Jürgen Becker ("Felder", 1964, and "Ränder", 1968), Rolf Dieter Brinkmann ("Keiner weiß mehr, 1968), Alexander Kluge ("Lebensläufe", 1962, and "Schlachtbeschreibung", 1964), and Dieter Wellershoff "Ein schöner Tag", 1966, and "Die Schattengrenze", 1969). Such trends were cut across by "Concrete Poetry" (Helmut Heissenbüttel, Ernst Jandl, Franz Mon among others), who attempted to disregard the contents of linguistic communication, emphasising formal traditions and taking the material character of language as their starting-point. Literature and its process of production thus becomes the theme, and language the object of literature.

The 1960s did not only bring the politisation of literature, they also brought a new self-assurance on the part of writers. Authors proclaimed the "end of self-effacement" (Heinrich Böll), and in 1969 set up the German Writers' Association (Verband Deutscher Schriftsteller) which joined the "Print and Paper" trade union in 1973. This union allegiance, which was only rejected by a minority of authors grouped in the Free German Authors' Association, was aimed at furthering implementation of demands for welfare provisions for writers' old age, at abolition of regulations permitting the unrestricted use of texts, free of charge, for school books, at public lending rights for authors, and at improvement of contracts with publishers – demands whose justification has been demonstrated, above all, by the Enquiry into Authors' Situation (Der Autorenreport, 1972), commissioned by the Federal Government.

The "Kursbuch 15" (1968) announced the "death of literature" because it contributed nothing to solution of unacceptable social and political circumstances. In the 1970s, however, "Belles Lettres" flourished as never before. Politisation was followed by a de-politisation, which was nevertheless in no way unpolitical. Instead the literature of this period of blocked reforms became a medium concerned with individual (political) experience even if not with complex political problems any longer. The "New Subjectivity" and the "New Sensibility" have, however, always run the danger of degenerating into mere self-preening.

This turn towards the individual, his rediscovery as a subject for literature, is particularly apparent in the novel – in autobiographical self-reassurance (Max Frisch, "Diaries 1966–1971", 1972. "Man in the Holocene", 1979. Wolfgang Koeppen, "Jugend", 1976. Thomas Bernhard, "Die Ursache", "Der Keller", and "Der Atem", 1975–78. Peter Handke, "Das Gewicht der Welt", 1977. Elias Canetti, "The Tongue Set Free", 1977), in the reflection of everyday political experience (Heinrich Böll, "The Lost Honour of Katharina Blum", 1974, and "Fürsorgliche Belagerung" 1979. Peter C. Chotjewitz, "Die Herren des Morgengrauens", 1978. Peter Schneider, "Lenz", 1973, and " . . . schon bist du ein Verfassungsfeind, 1977), and in the semi-documentary depiction of an individual artist (Peter Härtling, "Hölderlin", 1976. Wolfgang Hildesheimer, "Mozart", 1977. Adolf Muschg, "Gottfried Keller", 1977. Dieter Kühn, "Ich Wolkenstein", 1977). Retrospective reflection on individuality and development of an identity were central themes in women's literature of the Seventies (Karin Struck, "Klassenliebe", 1973. "Die Mutter", 1975. Verena Stefan, "Häutungen", 1975. Brigitte Schwaiger, "Wie kommt das Salz ins Meer?", 1977). The poetry (Jürgen Theobaldy, Wolf Wondratschek, and Nicolas Born) and drama of this period (Botho Strauß, "Trilogie des Wiedersehens", 1976, and

"Groß und klein", 1978) were even more concerned than the novel with reflection of everyday reality. Exceptional sensitivity to psychological processes is usually accompanied here by precise and detailed description of the banal everyday.

Some statistics, dates, and names with reference to literary life in the Federal Republic of Germany will complement the foregoing short survey of post-war writing.

According to the "Report on Authors", which provides the most recent available figures, there were in 1972 some 7,200 self-employed authors and translators. Book production can be ascertained in the statistics issued annually by the German Book Trade. In 1977 some 40,000 new titles were published, and almost 10,000 books produced in new editions. Paperback production attained almost 6,500 titles. The average shop price of all these books was 21.87 DM. Around 2,300 publishers were in existence in that year. These included publishers producing only works of scholarship, firms concentrating on school books, big companies catering for mass taste such as Bertelsmann, Droemer, Molden, and Schneekluth, the more exclusively literary publishers (S. Fischer, Carl Hanser, Luchterhand, Kiepenheuer & Witsch, Rowohlt, Suhrkamp, and Wagenbach), and the big publishers of paperbacks (Deutscher Taschenbuch Verlag, Fischer, Goldmann, Heyne, Rowohlt, and Ullstein). These publishers' turnover amounted to 6.1 milliard DM, the intermediate book trade took 2.7 milliard DM, and general booksellers 2.4 milliard DM. These figures do not contain the earnings of book clubs, of which the biggest and most important are the Bertelsmann Lesering, the Deutsche Buchgemeinschaft, the Europäische Bildungsgemeinschaft, and the Büchergilde Gutenberg. A special part is played in the many ways and means of mediating literature by literary magazines (Akzente, Die Horen, Hermannstrasse 14, Literaturmagazin, and Tintenfisch), the arts sections of the daily and weekly press, and programmes on writing and culture in radio and television. The advancement of literature is served by stipendia (Villa Massimo, and the Federal Association of German Industry), literary prizes (Georg Büchner Prize, Alfred Döblin Prize, Petrarca Prize, and the German Book Trade's Peace Prize), and by academies, archives, and literary societies, which have often at the same time taken on such functions as the collecting and ordering of writers' literary bequest (Akademie der Künste, Berlin. Akademie der Wissenschaften und der Literatur, Mainz. Bayerische Akademie der Schönen Künste, Munich. Deutsche Akademie für Sprache und Dichtung, Darmstadt. Deutsches Literaturarchiv/Schiller-Nationalmuseum, Marbach am Neckar. Freies Deutsches Hochstift, Frankfurt. Goethe-Museum, Düsseldorf. Herzog-August-Bibliothek, Wolfenbüttel).

Günther Fetzer

Important German authors from the period between the two World Wars. From l. to r.: Hermann Hesse (1877–1962), Gottfried Benn (1886–1956), Erich Kästner (1899–1974) talking to Carl Zuckmayer (1896–1977), and Bertolt Brecht (1898–1956).

A meeting of the literature section of the Prussian Academy of Arts at Berlin in 1930. Standing from l.: Bernhard Kellermann (1879–1951), Alfred Döblin (1878–1957), Thomas Mann (1875–1955), Max Halbe (1865–1944), Seated: Hermann Stehr (1864–1940), Alfred Mombert (1872–1942), Eduard Stucken (1865–1936), Wilhelm von Scholz (1874–1969), Oskar Loerke (1884–1941), Walter von Molo (1880–1958), Ludwig Fulda (1862–1939), Heinrich Mann (1871–1950).

The cover of "Verbannte und Verbrannte" ("Banned and Burned"), an anthology by German-speaking emigrés published in London in 1942.

A scene from "The Man Outside", the tragedy of a man returning home after the war by Wolfgang Borchert (1921–1947).

Important contemporary German authors – from l. to r.: Heinrich Böll (b. 1917), Siegfried Lenz (b. 1926), Wolfgang Koeppen (b. 1906), and Wolfgang Hildesheimer (b. 1916).

Günther Eich (1907–1972)

Important titles in recent years.

1966

1959

Paul Celan (1920–1970)

Important titles in recent years.

1967

1969

1973

1973

Arno Schmidt (1914–1979), novelist, literary critic, and translator, in front of his house at Bargfeld, Schleswig-Holstein.

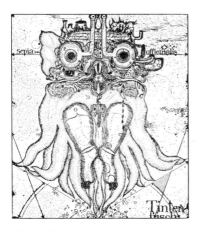

"Tintenfisch", a literary yearbook, has been published by the Verlag Klaus Wagenbach in West Berlin since 1968. The engraving for the cover of the 3rd issue was by Uwe Bremer.

The celebrated 1966 Princeton meeting of the "Gruppe 47" established at Munich in 1947 by Hans Werner Richter. From the right: literary scholar Hans Mayer, and poet Erich Fried.

The April 1978 annual meeting of the German section of the PEN Club at Erlangen. From the left: Thaddäus Troll, Walter Jens (the organisation's chairman), and new members Reiner Kunze and Heinz Piontek.

Heinrich Böll received the Nobel Prize for Literature at Stockholm on September 12, 1972. The prize committee spoke of his work having contributed towards a renewal of German literature through combining a broad spectrum of insights of contemporary relevance with the sensibility of creative powers. In the photo from r. to l.: Heinrich Böll, the then Swedish Crown-Prince Carl Gustav, Margarete of Denmark, and Princess Christina of Sweden.

"Immer so durchgemogelt – Erinnerungen an unsere Schulzeit", the latest work by *Walter Kempowski (b. 1929) who earns his living as a teacher, tells of his own schooldays.*

Günter Grass at a meeting of the German Writers' Association.

Contemporary women writers in German. From l. to r.: Ilse Aichinger, Marie Luise Kaschnitz, Angelika Mechtel, Karin Struck, Gabriele Wohmann.

The literary periodicals act alongside newspaper review sections and magazine book pages as an important intermediary between authors and the reading public. The periodicals depicted here stand for many others. "Hermannstraße 14", Verlag Klett-Cotta, Stuttgart; "Literatur-Magazin", Rowohlt Taschenbuch Verlag, Reinbek, near Hamburg; "Tintenfisch", Verlag Klaus Wagenbach, West Berlin; "Text und Kritik", Boorberg Verlag, Munich; "Akzente", Carl Hanser Verlag, Munich; "Merkur", Klett-Cotta, Stuttgart.

An extensive network of libraries, large and small, provides people in all parts of the Federal Republic with access to books. The photo (right) shows one of the most celebrated of these libraries, the Herzog-August-Bibliothek at Wolfenbüttel in Lower Saxony. Gotthold Ephraim Lessing was librarian there from 1770 to 1781.

The interior of the Prussian State Library opened at West Berlin in 1979.

The still unsurpassed model of book production – the 42 line, double column Latin Bible set by Johannes Gutenberg in 1455.

The "International Museum for the Art of Printing" at Gutenberg's birthplace, Mainz on the Rhine, fulfils an important function in preserving the book as an art-form. The photo shows a demonstration of printing on a replica of Johannes Gutenberg's hand-press.

The "Frankfurt Book Fair" is the annual highpoint for authors, translators, and producers and sellers of books from all over the world. In 1980 there were 5,216 publishing firms from 95 countries presenting a total of 285,000 book titles, 86,000 of which were new publications. A view of one of the exhibition halls.

Illustrations are particularly important in books for children and young people. The photo shows a picture from Ursula Wölfel's "Ein Tapir im Dorf" by Bettina Anrich-Wölfel. This appears as one of the two-language children's books published by the Verlag Jugend und Volk, Munich.

Provision is made for tomorrow's reader by way of competitions linked with readings, exhibitions of books for the young, presentations such as "How a book is made" (above), and by well-developed libraries for young people, especially in towns. The photo below shows a travelling library at work.

Five pre-war German artists stand for the proscribed generation. From l. to r.: Max Beckmann (1884–1950), August Macke (1887–1914), Käthe Kollwitz (1867–1945), Emil Nolde (1867–1956), Ernst Ludwig Kirchner (1880–1938).

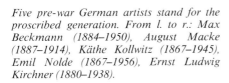

The visual arts

Artistic creativity in the Federal Republic of Germany has attained an impressive range and diversity in the course of thirty years. It has become increasingly integrated in the international scene, taking over foreign influences whilst at the same time preserving fundamental elements within national forms of thought and expression.

The 1950s were devoted to an endeavour to fill the spiritual and creative vacuum left by the destructive "cultural policy" under National Socialism. Re-establishing links with older traditions, artists were particularly attracted by Expressionism (HAP Grieshaber, Werner Gilles, Eduard Bargheer, Werner Heldt), the myths of nature to be found in Surrealism (Richard Oelze), or the teachings of the Bauhaus. They also sought intensive contacts with Paris, which after the Second World War once again became, for a decade, a focus for international art. E.W. Nay, Georg Meistermann, and Hann Trier thus developed their individual forms of Abstract Expressionism, whilst the Frankfurt "Quadriga" (Bernhard Schultze, Karl Otto Götz, Otto Greis, Heinz Kreutz), the "53 Group" from Düsseldorf (including Gerhard Hoehme and Peter Brüning), and a number of outstanding individualists such as Emil Schumacher, Karl Fred Dahmen, or K.R.H. Sonderborg pursued art informel or Tachisme.

The tradition of decentralisation of artistic life continued to prevail in the Federal Republic of Germany. This was promoted – rather than in any way infringed upon – by the federal structure of the state and by the cultural ambitions of the *Laender.* Academies and other art schools were thus able to attract teachers with a high reputation, who in turn drew in students. West Berlin, Hamburg, Munich (for Bavaria), Stuttgart and Karlsruhe (for Baden-Württemberg), and Frankfurt/Main and Kassel (for Hesse) were all celebrated sources of training, but the list was headed by Düsseldorf (North Rhine-Westphalia) whose Academy with its long-established traditions provided the Federal German art scene with an important part of the reputation it enjoys today. It also seems that there will be little change in that respect in the near future.

It was also at Düsseldorf in the winter of 1957/58 that the "Zero Group" (Otto Piene, Heinz Mack, Günter Uecker) became the first German art movement to appear since the war to really produce something new and soon to serve as an inspiration abroad. Taking as their starting-point discoveries in the monochrome and the meditative by Rupprecht Geiger, Almir Mavignier, Lothar Quinte, and Yves Klein from France, the "Zero Group" introduced external spaces into the creative process by means of light, air, smoke, fire, and water. The logical next step, which followed soon afterwards, was the transition to mobile art and kinetics (Heinz Mack, Harry Kramer, Günter Haese, Hermann Goepfert, Hartmut Böhm).

It was once again in Düsseldorf that Konrad Klapheck in 1955 created a typewriter in "prosaic super-realism", thus taking a first step towards artistic retrieval of tangible reality. It may be true that this did not exert any immediate impact since most German artists and the public were still largely fixated on Abstraction but Klapheck's breakthrough was also to be international when just before the mid-1960s American Pop Art rolled over the artistic landscape of the Federal Republic of Germany, forcing its way into private galleries and collections, into exhibition halls and museums, making realistic art acceptable once again. Pop Art did not exert a great stylistic influence on Federal German artists though.

Constructivism, which had already been written off as finished, experienced a revival in the 1960s in conjunction with devotion of renewed attention to the achievements of the Twenties. Max Bill from Switzerland and Josef Albers, who had emigrated to the USA decades earlier, became the new models. This led to development of colourful geometrical art (Günter Fruhtrunk, Karl Georg Pfahler, Winfred Gaul, Helmut Sundhaußen), Op and Serial Art (Leo Breuer, Adolf Luther, Ludwig Wilding, Peter Roehr), new forms of objects (Franz Rudolf Knubel, Utz Kampmann), and a Minimal Art reduced to simple basic elements (Erwin Heerich).

Abstract and realistic tendencies were almost equally predominant on the German art scene in the second half of the 1960s. Between these two poles there developed entire ranges of new forms of expression whose differentiation and reciprocal superimposition both produced a flourishing pluralism and suspended possibilities of relatively precise stylistic categorisation as had previously existed.

At that time it was possible for a great diversity of tendencies to find a place within the work of a single artist. An example of that is provided by Gerhard Richter who moved from figurative art and depictions of nature to abstract washes and works close to Op Art. This painter became known for his ironically blurred paraphrases of real situations taken from amateur photographs, postcards, and advertising prospectuses, thus providing a new kind of legitimation for employing photos in art.

Most realists – and particularly painters like Fritz Köthe, Peter Klasen, Malte Sartorius, and Karolus Lodenkämper, who constitute the core of the Photo-Realists – naturally work with objects that can be photographed. It is worthy of note though that thematic emphases, linked with specific regions and even towns, are apparent among the realists to a greater extent than is the case with representatives of other artistic styles. Magical figurative realism dominates in the Rhineland (Karl Heidelbach, Dieter Kraemer, Lothar Braun, Jobst Meyer, Hans-Peter Reuter) and in Hamburg (where Dieter Asmus, Peter Nagel, Nikolaus Störtenbecker, and Dietmar Ullrich established the "Zebra Group" in 1965), whereas Critical Realism is centred on West Berlin (Ulrich Baehr, H.J. Diehl, Peter Sorge, Wolfgang Petrick, Jürgen Waller, Maina-Miriam Munsky, Johannes Grützke).

It can hardly seem surprising that a critical spirit flourishes in this city. That is local tradition – with the democratic artists community of the 1919 November Group, the social criticism of the Verismus of George Grosz and Otto Dix, and the final refuge of the Bauhaus artists. Current geo-political circumstances, the city's island situation, also makes people more perceptive. Two of the most prominent forms of political realism are, nevertheless, to be found in the Federal Republic itself – Klaus Staeck's aggressive posters and collages of graphics and text, and Siegfried Neuenhausen's material objects, frequently depicting oppressed human beings whose anonymity even intensifies this denunciation of all repression and the accompanying immanent appeal to morality and reason.

This retrieval of optically perceptible reality was by no means a source of inspiration merely to realists. It also inspired the even larger circle of artists whose work is seen as part of the New Figuration. Mention should be made in this context of Horst Antes with his flat torsoless figures, of Rainer Küchenmeister's phantom figures, Dieter Krieg's combinations of people and ornamentation, and of the sensitive drawn psychogrammes by Horst Janssen and Rudolf Schoofs. They also have much in common with such painters of schematised landscapes as Bernd Koberling, Werner Nöfer, and Jens Lausen.

From the early Sixties, Happenings and Fluxus perhaps most decisively called into question the visual arts' traditional forms of depiction. Both aimed at the staging of an action with participation by the public rather than at the creation of a work of art. This Action Art was taken over from America as a "flowing unity of art and life", and became particularly associated with the names of Wolf Vostell and Joseph Beuys. Both were also involved in the transition from Actions to Performance where direct participation by the public was dropped in favour of visualisation of relationships to space and time in carefully thought-through sequences of events. The people involved included Klaus Rinke, Michael Buthe, Jürgen Klauke, Jochen Gerz, Friederike Petzold, Rebecca Horn, and Ulrike Rosenbach, who were mostly also active in the sphere of Photo- and Video Art.

Beuys is, without any doubt, the most internationally celebrated German artist today. He has introduced perishable substances such as lard and honey (as sources of energy) and felt (as an insulating material) into art. These materials and a theoretical superstructure serving an evolutionary ideology evoke many kinds of associations, and also extend the social and political dimensions of the concept of art. Beuys is at any rate a striking representative of that emphasis on the individual characterising art in the Federal Republic of Germany at the end of the 1970s.

From the early Sixties onwards, that development was accompanied by constantly mounting public interest. That received expression in both increasing attendance at exhibitions of contemporary art, and in an absolute boom in the establishment of private galleries. In places where previously there had been perhaps three or four people dealing in modern art, ten, twenty, or even forty galleries (in cities like Cologne and Düsseldorf) sprang up overnight. In West Berlin there are almost twice as many galleries.

The first market for contemporary art was held at Cologne in 1967. That was such a success that this model was soon followed elsewhere, particularly in other Western European countries. For artists that meant a considerable improvement in possibilities of showing their works, and thus a greater chance of receiving attention from art critics in daily newspapers, local radio, or art magazines as well as the prospect of being able to sell their works. The number of individual customers and small-scale collectors of contemporary art has considerably increased since then. The interest of the big collectors, which previously seldom extended beyond the modern classics, is now more clearly directed towards the current scene.

The museums are of course the most coveted purchasers of art as far as artists and gallery-owners are concerned. There are some 50 state or municipal institutions with sections for modern art or collections devoted solely to modern art in the Federal Republic of Germany today. Contemporary art is either constantly or spasmodically on show in over 260 museums, big art galleries, and art associations. It is not thought relevant whether the artists concerned are German or not.

Despite this situation though, it is just not the case that a considerable number of artists have achieved commercial prosperity. That is largely an outcome of the fact that there are very many more artists today than in former times to share the existing market with foreigners.

Artists are therefore, despite the increase in public recognition, more dependent than ever on some kind of a safety-net. For most of them that means a second job, most frequently as art teacher. The consequence for the public authorities is that a constant effort must be made to improve artists' welfare. The preconditions for that were laid down in the enquiry into the situation facing artists carried out on behalf of the Federal Ministry of Labour and Social Structure and published in 1975 as the "Künstler-Report". That led to agreement, with the support of artists' and art dealers' professional groupings, on contractual arrangements covering introduction of additional protection for copyright and of welfare deductions so as to provide benefits for artists.

Federal, regional, and municipal authorities are still obliged to spend up to 2 % of the construction costs of public buildings on their embellishment by artists and craftsmen. The extent of public or publicly subsidised building means that this regulation is particularly important, not least in terms of the long-term impact for artists whose work is thus open to public view and subject to discussion.

Public subsidies are the rule in the Federal Republic of Germany for exhibitions instigated or backed by the cultural authorities. That applies to local and regional presentations as well as to such outstanding events as the "documenta", which has taken place at Kassel every four or five years since 1955. This exhibition is viewed as being of seismographic significance with regard to trends and developments in the current art scene all over the world. It is financed by the town of Kassel, the *Land* of Hesse, and the Federal authorities. Subsidies are also available so as to enable German artists to participate in such foreign exhibitions as the Biennale at Venice and São Paulo, or in individual or travelling shows of contemporary German art, arranged under the auspices of bilateral cultural agreements. Scholarships enable German artists to pursue their studies for a limited period at Rome (Villa Massimo), Florence (Villa Romana), and, more recently, New York where the holders (from West Berlin, Düsseldorf, and Cologne) can move into studios in a former school – usually for a year with financial assistance from their home city. The *Laender,* local authorities, institutions, and private foundations in the Federal Republic of Germany also award over 80 art prizes and scholarships annually on top of their purchases of art. Competitions are held too. Information about such matters is contained in the "Handbuch

der Kulturpreise und der individuellen Künstlerförderung in der Bundesrepublik Deutschland" (Cologne 1978) produced on behalf of the
Federal Ministry of the Interior. Mention should also be made of the
nationwide representation of German artists in the Bundesverband
bildender Künstler and the Deutscher Künstlerbund, and in a large
number of regional and local groupings dedicated to the further
development of contemporary art. Finally, reference should also be
made to the plan for artists to receive an annual sum out of the funds
collected for a National Foundation. A start was made there in 1980.

Horst Richter

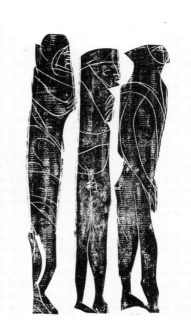

HAP Grieshaber (b. 1909) whose work focuses almost entirely on the woodcut. His "Columns" date from 1948.

Horst Janssen (b. 1929) made his name with drawings and engravings. His etching "Klee and Ensor Disputing Over a Kipper" was produced in 1961.

Trunkless figures, constantly varied, are the trademark of Horst Antes (b. 1936). "King", 1967. Aquatec.

The main theme in the paintings and lithographs of Paul Wunderlich (b. 1927) is man reduced to his physicality in a dialectical relationship between beauty and deformation. The picture here is simply entitled "Gouache".

*Bernard Schultze (b. 1915) pro-
duces pictures and sculptural
works in the style of Tachisme.
L.: his painted sculpture "With a
hand", 1966*

*Johannes Schreiter (b. 1930) con-
centrates on "Fire collages" (a
technique he has developed), and
on stained glass painting. The
photo shows a window in the altar
area of the Protestant Church of
St. John in the Lehe district of
Bremerhaven (1965).*

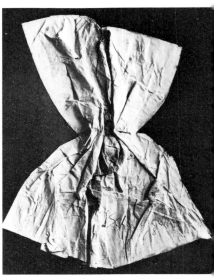

Colour – as material existence and psychic impact – is the theme of the work of Emil Schumacher (b. 1912). His creations are characterised by disruptions of composition and of the colour used. Schumacher utilised paper, acrylic, and canvas for his "Paper Doll" (1968).

Painter Karl Fred Dahmen (b. 1917) has crossed the traditional boundaries between painting and sculpture in his search for new possibilities of depiction. The artist used various materials in his "Corsett picture" (1965).

*The most successful but at the same time most controversial German artist of the
1970s was Joseph Beuys. In 1979 he became the first living German artist to be
honoured with a retrospective at New York's Guggenheim Museum.*

*An "Action" by Joseph Beuys (b. 1921). In 1972 the leading eccentric in the
German avantgarde had himself paddled across the Rhine in a dugout at
Düsseldorf.*

*Monschau Castle and the Haller ruins dating from the 14th century were wrapped
in plastic sheeting in accordance with the instructions of Bulgarian-born "Packa-
ging Artist" Christo now resident in the Federal Republic. This was part of the
1971 Open-Air Exhibition at Monschau in North Rhine-Westphalia.*

The "Contact Art" group of sculptors produce their works in public, actively including spectators. The photos show (l. to r.): "ell-bench", sculpture for climbing by Otto Almstadt and Moritz Bormann, Bremen 1974. Moritz Bormann during Contact Art activities at Hanover in 1973. Bremen children with works that they themselves produced during such activities at Bremen in 1974. "Motivation" of an object by Bernd Uiberall in Bremen (1974). A 1973 presentation by the Contact Group at Hanover in 1973.

Artistic creation as a form of work therapy. Inmates of a Bremen prison producing sculpture.

Rebecca Horn devises objects intended to spark off processes of self-identification among their users. The photos show her "Mechanical Body Fans".

"Living sculptures" was the name given by Munich Action Artist Hanna Frenzel to her highly diverse presentations – in this case in front of Munich's Glyptothek.

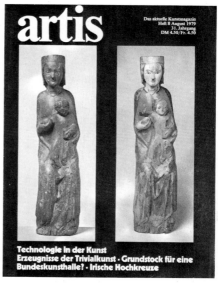

Covers of important art magazines in the Federal Republic. Below right: "das kunstjahrbuch", an important source of information about events in the Federal Republic of Germany, Austria, and Switzerland.

In January 1979, the Minister of the Interior, Gerhart Baum (l.), authorised the purchase of seven sculptures by Surrealist Max Ernst (1891–1976). 1,180,000 DM from the budget for general promotion of art were used to buy this collection for the projected Federal Art Gallery at Bonn.

An example of the "Art on Buildings" programme supported by state assistance. The facade of a faculty building at Freiburg University in Baden-Württemberg.

Further examples of art on buildings. Above: sculpture by Erich Hauser in front of the Baden-Württemberg official representation in Bonn – steel, c. 9 m. high, 1973. Below: sculpture by Hans Uhlmann in front of the Deutsche Oper, West Berlin, c. 20 m. hight, 1961.

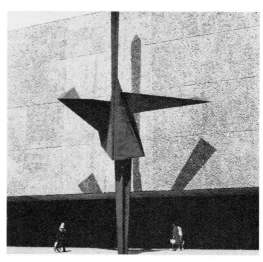

"Journey into the sea" – a project by Hannsjörg Voth. In October 1976 the artist completed initial construction plans for his "dynamic sculpture", which on the 30th of May 1978 was floated down the Rhine from Ludwigshafen via Rotterdam to the sea where it was burnt on June 5th.

Underwater experimental art. Jürgen Claus's "La Parra-Blume" with diver, 1974.

An important representative of the "Critical Realism" group – Dieter Asmus, "Girl at the seaside", 1976, serigraphic, 56 x 68 cm.

Political art – Klaus Staeck with a poster campaign in Nuremberg, 1971. This utilisation of Dürer's mother was intended to focus attention on social injustices. His text runs: Would you let a room to this woman?

Würden Sie dieser Fräulein Zimmer vermieten?

An example of Photo-Realism – Gerhard Richter, "Landscape with small bridge, Hubbelrath", 1969, oil on canvas, 120 x 150 cm.

"documenta" is the name of the celebrated international exhibitions that have been held, at irregular intervals, at Kassel/Hesse since 1955. The photo shows Hans-Peter Reuter's tile construction "Space Object" at documenta 6 in 1977.

Museums and exhibitions

For German museums and exhibitions, tradition extends back to the early 19th century when city and state museums were set up alongside princely collections which had already existed for a considerable time, and when civic initiatives led to the establishment of art societies whose main function consisted of the organisation of exhibitions.

Museums devoted to art and cultural history were soon complemented by museums concerned with natural history and technology, and alongside the big institutions which quickly gained an international reputation there were a large number of smaller set-ups, mainly special collections and 'homeland' museums. Their number has increased since the founding of the Federal Republic of Germany, and continues to grow.

Today there are over 1,500 museums in the area covered by the Federal Republic of Germany and West Berlin. 63 % of these receive financial support from towns and regional bodies, and 23 % from the federal authorities and *Laender*. The other 14 % is accounted for by private set-ups open to the public, kept going by clubs, societies, foundations, churches, industry and commerce, and in individual cases by artists, their legatees, and collectors. Most of them receive regular public assistance. The greatest density of museums (300 in number) is in North Rhine-Westphalia, which is the most heavily populated of the *Laender.*

Many museums have the status of scholarly institutes with regard both to presentation of their own collections and to comparative research and teaching. In some cases their work is linked with the conservation of historic monuments.

Among the 14 most important state museums are the "Prussian Cultural Foundation" established by law to administer such West Berlin collections as the celebrated Dahlem Gallery (for classical painting) and the National Gallery (for modern art), the Germanic National Museum at Nuremberg as the most important source for German artistic and cultural history, and Munich's German Museum, the largest European museum for the natural sciences and technology. All these top-ranking museums have the legal structure of foundations or public corporations, financed by the federal authorities and the *Laender*. Similar assistance is also available for the Central Roman-Germanic Museum at Mainz, the German Mining Museum at Bochum, the German Shipping Museum at Bremerhaven, and the Natural History Research Institute and Senckenberg Institute at Frankfurt/ Main.

Many of the museums supported by individual *Laender* are just as much of an international attraction. These include the Bavarian State Collections with the world-famous Alte Pinakothek and Glyptothek, the Neue Pinakothek, and the Gallery of Modern Art (all at Munich), the state galleries at Stuttgart and Karlsruhe (both Baden-Württemberg), the North Rhine-Westphalia collection at Düsseldorf, the Kassel state collection (Hesse), the Hesse Museum at Darmstadt, the Rhenish Museum at Trier (Rhineland-Palatinate), the Duke Anton Ulrich Museum at Brunswick (Lower Saxony), the Lower Saxony Museum at Hanover, and the Schleswig-Holstein Museum at Schleswig. The Bremen Overseas Museum and the Hamburg Art Museum are financed by the city-states involved, and responsibility for the collections at Veste Coburg and the regional museums at Bonn and Münster lies with local bodies (the Coburg Foundation, and the Rhineland and Westphalia-Lippe Associations).

Particularly worthy of mention are the art museums at Hanover (including the Sprengel collection), Essen (Folkwang Museum), Duisburg (Wilhelm Lehmbruck Museum), Wuppertal (Von der Heydt Museum), and Munich (Municipal Gallery in the Lenbachhaus).

The city of Cologne disposes over the most extensive art collections in the care of a local authority. These nine collections include the Wallraf Richartz Museum (mainly painting up to 1900), and the Ludwig Museum of Modern Art. All these urban establishments were originally set up by local citizens, and that is true of the majority of museums in the Federal Republic of Germany. In many cases these citizens both donated the collections and also financed the construction of museums.

A number of museums are maintained by the Churches or ecclesiastical bodies, and these include the Archiepiscopal Diocesan Museums at Paderborn and Cologne, and the German Bible Foundation's Bible Museum at Stuttgart.

Larger private museums can now virtually only be kept in existence by industry in the form of foundations as in the case of the Herbig-Haarhaus Paint Museum at Cologne, the German Playing Cards Museum at

Leinfelden-Echterdingen, or the Ernst Barlach House at Hamburg. The first museum to be set up by local citizens – the Städelsche Art Institute at Frankfurt/Main in 1816 – is now largely dependent on public funds.

Private foundations and donations by individuals and groups continue though to constitute an important, and sometimes the chief, element in financing a large number of museums whose budgets are too limited to permit more extensive acquisitions. Well-founded appeals by these institutions to the public authorities (particularly regional and local parliaments) seldom go unheard but private patrons are usually more flexible.

These private patrons are headed by "Associations of Friends and Patrons" primarily set up to gather donations, which also organise lectures, film evenings, and excursions for the museums. They also include firms from industry and commerce which are members of the previously mentioned Associations and fulfil museums' wishes in commemoration of business jubilees. There are also the lottery organisations which transform their surpluses into cultural donations to museums, radio and television stations which give to museums part of their earnings from advertising programmes, and specially organised civic initiatives calling for public donations to mark some special museum occasion such as an anniversary, the opening of new rooms, or a change in directors.

Karl Ernst Osthaus (Hagen), Josef Haubrich (Cologne), Bernhard Sprengel (Hanover), Wilhelm Hack (Cologne/Ludwigshafen), and Karl Ströher (Darmstadt) have made a name for themselves as patrons in the grand style by transforming their private art collections into public property. The main person to be mentioned in this connection though is Peter Ludwig, the owner of an Aachen chocolate factory, who works together with 17 museums in the Federal Republic of Germany and abroad by endowing them with long-term loans. Part of the Ludwig collection will be housed in the museum now being constructed alongside Cologne cathedral, and due to open in 1985.

During the Second World War many places fortunately succeeded in storing their museum collections away from danger, thus preventing extensive losses. The museum buildings themselves mostly became rubble and ashes. After establishment of the Federal Republic of Germany, almost all *Laender* and cities were faced with the task of rebuilding institutes that had been destroyed, and making those that had been damaged usable again. That could not happen immediately since the priorities in this process of general reconstruction lay initially with houses, schools, welfare facilities, and administrative buildings. The re-establishment of opera houses, theatres, and concert halls was also a fairly high priority. Only after that did the public planners turn their attention to museums. Making good losses and providing for new needs took place fairly quickly though, thanks to a considerable extent to an appeal by the German Research Association in 1971 and its "Memorandum on the situation of museums" in 1974.

Thirty years after the Federal Republic of Germany came into being, it is clear that the damage done to the country's museums has been put to rights wherever possible, and that there has even been a boom in new museum buildings, which would previously have scarcely been conceivable. The federal structure of cultural life in West Germany helped ensure that this development was not restricted to a few geographical areas but benefitted all the *Laender* according to their populations. Apart from the hundreds of restored museums, there were new establishments which for the most part soon had buildings of their own. Space limits mention here to Regensburg's East German Gallery (1970) in Bavaria, Ludwigshafen's Wilhelm Hack Museum (1979) in Rhineland Palatinate, Saarbrücken's Modern Gallery (1968) in the Saarland, and the Hanover Art Museum (1979) in Lower Saxony. Museum-opening was most apparent in North Rhine-Westphalia with Dortmund's Ostwall Museum (1949), the Recklinghausen Art Gallery (1950) closely linked with the Ruhr Festival, Leverkusen's Schloß Morsbroich (1951), Bonn's City Museum (1954), the Bochum Museum (1960), the North Rhine-Westphalia Art Collection at Düsseldorf (1961), Duisburg's Wilhelm Lehmbruck Museum (1964), the Bielefeld Art Gallery (1968), the Aachen City Gallery (1970), and the "Quadrat Bottrop" (1976). The planning and realisation of these buildings were discussed by the general public as well as by experts to a remarkable extent – especially the museums at Neuss and Mönchengladbach, the Roman-Germanic and East Asian Museums at Cologne, the Stuttgart State Gallery, the New Pinakothek in Munich, and the Museum of Ethnology and the Bauhaus Archive in West Berlin. The same is true of extensive new projects in Cologne and Frankfurt/Main, and particularly of the plan to establish a Federal Art Gallery at Bonn. Federal interests and the cultural autonomy of the *Laender* come into contact here.

The museum boom has been accompanied by a boom in attendance, which is no less astonishing. The annual total for visits to museums and public exhibitions in the Federal Republic amounted to around 17 million at the end of the 1960s. This increased to 22 million by 1975, and shot up to no less than 38.5 million in 1979. That means that attendance more than doubled within a decade. For statisticians of culture it is a great surprise to find that considerably more people now visit museums and exhibitions than go to football matches (18 million) and theatres (20 million).

This upsurge in attendance was brought about by new ideas about the museum, democratisation of cultural activities, improvements in presentation of exhibits and collections, and by an educational emphasis on accessibility. Other factors were involved too. An important part was played by general activation of what became known as the leisure society, and by the spread of all levels of schooling and academic education resulting in an expanded demand for culture. New sections of the public were reached by way of art fairs and markets, particularly in the Rhineland, and also as a result of often very comprehensive reports in the mass media – daily and weekly newspapers, illustrated magazines, radio, and television. All that accounts for the constant increase in attendance at the "documenta" exhibition of contemporary art, held every four or five years at Kassel, or at presentations of the work of individual artists such as Max Ernst (Munich/West Berlin), Salvadore Dali (Baden-Baden), and Ernst Ludwig Kirchner (West Berlin/Cologne/Munich).

That also applies to an even greater extent to the comprehensive exhibitions and the historical retrospectives, which have been presented more frequently than ever before since the early 1970s. "World Cultures and Modern Art", shown during the 1972 Munich Olympic Games where it attracted 200,000 people, was an important turning-point in this programme. It was followed by "Rhine and Meuse – Art and Culture 800–1400" at Cologne in 1973 (attendance 220,000), the extensive Art Nouveau exhibition at Darmstadt in 1976 (600,000), "The Age of the Hohenstaufen" at Stuttgart in 1977 (800,000), the fifteenth Council of Europe exhibition at West Berlin in 1977 devoted to "Trends in the Twenties" (345,000), and "The Parlers – European art under the Luxemburgs" at Cologne in 1978 (300,000). Over 430,000 people attended the highly successful "Art around 1800" cycle of exhibitions started by the Hamburg Art Gallery in 1974. These presentations have included "Caspar David Friedrich" and "William Turner and the Landscape of his Age".

Among the exhibitions that regularly attract high attendances and a great deal of attention from the mass media are presentations devoted to the culture of other peoples and continents such as Thracian Gold from

Bulgaria, Tutankhamen from Egypt, the Numidians from the Maghreb region of North Africa, the Pre-Columbian treasures of Latin America, the Indians of North America, works of Buddhist art from the main areas of origin, and monuments of Far Eastern art. The interest aroused by mass tourism has a gratifying impact here.

The time is past when museums were mainly concerned with the needs of the so-called "educated classes", and were almost synonymous with boredom and dreariness. Museums in the Federal Republic of Germany are integrated in society as a whole and fulfil important functions there, extending far beyond what is traditionally associated with such institutions. These new functions include such artistic activities as Happenings and Performances, the showing of artists' films and video experiments, educational work such as children's painting schools and adult education classes, and practical demonstrations of restoration etc. Museums are increasingly serving as locations for leisure activities, as places for avantgarde music and participatory culture.

The space, technical facilities, and staff available to organisations devoted to the collection and exhibition of art have not kept pace with constant expansion of museum collections and mounting numbers of visitors. There is also not enough practical training available for museum staff at all levels. Initial steps have, however, been taken to improve the situation. A Museums Institute has been established by the Prussian Cultural Foundation in West Berlin, and the Rhineland Regional Association has set up a museum school in the former Brauweiler Abbey near Cologne. Both institutes intend to impart knowledge about such matters as museum didactics, legal issues, administration, techniques, restoration, exhibition practice, protection for collections, looking after the public, and public relations.

Most exhibitions are organised by public galleries and private art associations. The most important urban galleries without any associated collection are in Baden-Baden, Tübingen, Cologne, Düsseldorf, and West Berlin. There are differences in their exhibition programmes but they are mainly concerned with the modern classics, extending up to the 1970s.

The art associations, of which there are over 70 in the Federal Republic and West Berlin, are chiefly dedicated to promoting the contemporary art scene. The smaller associations have up to 800 members, the medium-sized up to 2,000, and the large ones up to 4,000. The Rhenish-Westphalian Art Association at Düsseldorf was founded in 1829. It is the oldest such body in existence, and today's largest with a membership of over 7,000. In return for an annual subscription, these associations provide their members (and those of similar organisations) with free entry to their own exhibitions and other events, and also offer a yearly possibility of buying graphics or objects chosen or commissioned from among the works of well-known artists, and then produced in sufficient numbers.

Artists usually have their first encounter with the public by way of private galleries of which there are around 600 in the Federal Republic of Germany and West Berlin. These are mainly concentrated in Düsseldorf, Cologne, West Berlin, and Munich. The gallery-owners devote almost as much attention to foreign as to German artists. Contacts abroad are frequently established by way of the intensive activities of foreign cultural institutes in the Federal Republic, or by way of mediator organisations receiving state assistance and of diplomats. The latter particularly applies to countries that are inadequately represented on the free international art market or even completely absent there. Private gallery-owners are ready to take considerable risks. Leaving aside the relatively few internationally celebrated concerns, which work together with similar set-ups in New York, Paris, London, or Milan, exchanging artists and exhibitions, most galleries devoted to the discovery of new artists and the presentation of unfamiliar art operate in the uncertain sphere ahead of the general art scene. The frequent outcome is that such galleries only have a short life. That does not, however, discourage other idealists from in turn establishing new galleries, and attempting to launch artists they think particularly worthwhile. Artistic existence in the private sector thus constantly regenerates itself, playing a crucial part in the vitality and diversity of the panorama of exhibitions in the Federal Republic of Germany.

Horst Richter

Painting courses for children form an important aspect of museum educational activities.

Art comes to the department store. Frankfurt's Saalburg Museum for Pre- and Early History attempted to reach untapped parts of the public by exhibiting Roman inscriptions in stone and sculptures in one of the city's big stores.

The 500 Late Gothic works of art from twenty European countries in the Cologne City Gallery's 1978/79 exhibition devoted to "The Parlers" attracted 300,000 visitors.

The West Berlin Academy of Arts, which presents concerts, film, theatre, and evenings of modern dance as well as exhibitions, was concerned in 1977 with "Trends in the Twenties". This new kind of exhibition, attempting to put across the portrait of an epoch's art, culture, and history, was a great success with the public, and has been adopted by many other museums in the Federal Republic.

Science in public. The West Berlin Futurology Institute and the Federal Environmental Office attempted to make our world comprehensible as an "interlinked system" in a travelling exhibition which has visited 10 cities in the Federal Republic and neighbouring countries since 1978. What is growth? How can processes of interaction between technology and the environment be ascertained? What is the significance of limits? Complex cybernetic interrelationships were demonstrated by way of everyday examples, and directly experienced through learning games.

The German Museum in Munich, set up in 1903 by Oskar von Miller, an engineer, is one of the world's great institutions devoted to technology and the natural sciences. Visitors have an opportunity to set technical equipment in motion and to study its functioning – a didactic concept that educationists are also attempting to apply to art collections and historical museums.

At Friedrichshafen on Lake Constance, where the first rigid airship left the ground on July 2nd 1900, the Zeppelin Museum invokes the history of these "flying cigars".

The former epoch of the Windjammer is preserved at the German Shipping Museum at Bremerhaven (Bremen).

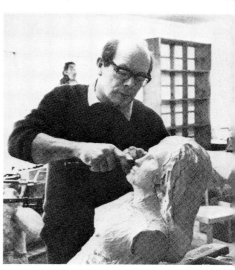

Practical demonstrations of craft techniques from the pre- and early industrial period – as here at the Schleswig–Holstein Open-Air Museum at Kiel – are also presented at many Historical and Homeland Museums.

Private collectors still help preserve the cultural legacy and promote contemporary art by their acquisitions and donations. The photo shows a model of the museum at present being built behind Cologne Cathedral (in the photo above r.) to house the Wallraf-Richartz-Museum and industrialist Peter Ludwig's collection of modern art.

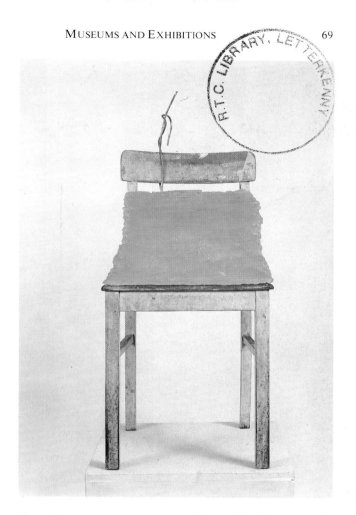

One of the pioneers among private collectors of modern art was the Darmstadt industrialist, Karl Ströher. He was also one of the first people to promote Joseph Beuys by buying his work. His collection is now on show at the Hesse Museum at Darmstadt. The photo shows Joseph Beuys' "Grease Chair" dating from 1964.

◄　*Ludwigshafen in Rhineland-Palatinate built a new museum to house its newly-acquired Wilhelm Hack collection with important works of Roman, Mediaeval, and 20th Century works of art. The photo shows the opening ceremony in the presence of the then Federal President, Walter Scheel, and the Prime Minister of Rhineland-Palatinate, Bernhard Vogel.*

One of the many large exhibitions that attracted the public in recent years was the Tutankhamen presentation at Cologne's City Museum. Between June 21 and October 19, 1980, more than 1.3 million people saw the Pharaoh's celebrated death-mask (see photo) and the other 54 artefacts on show. The exhibition had previously been in West Berlin, and moved on from Cologne to Munich.

Examples of thematically specialised collections. Above: hunting sledges and weapons at the German Hunting Museum in Munich. Below left: 16th century armour at the Cologne City Museum. Below right: Cabaret poster for "The 11 harsh judges" at Munich's Theatre Museum.

The "feudal legacy" of theatre in the Federal Republic of Germany – a view of the auditorium of the Old Residenztheater at Munich, also known as the "Cuvilliés Theatre" after its architect, François de Cuvilliés (1695–1768). This Rococco building was severely damaged during the Second World War, but it is now being used again by the Bavarian State Theatre and the Bavarian State Opera.

Cultural vitality in the Federal Republic of Germany can be experienced particularly well, perhaps even best of all, in the country's theatre. Its structure and diversity are exemplary, and the generous financial support it receives is unparalleled elsewhere in the world. At present the forces urging development and change may be powerful but German theatrical tradition has also remained strong.

Two historical turning-points exert a great influence on the present-day. Both occurred in the twentieth century, and both have ultimately done more for continuity than for radical reorientation. The tradition of the feudally-influenced court theatre, of the many urban theatres, extends far back into the eighteenth century. Its end seemed to have come, however, when the First World War put an end to the Kaiser's Reich and its principalities.

The public authorities got involved with the theatre though. Cities and states, represented by their parliaments, took on the provision of support as if that were a matter of course. During that time there developed in the Weimar Republic what is today the broadly-based German theatre system, which on the one hand is subsidised by the *Laender* and local authorities, and on the other guarantees a great deal of independence and individual responsibility to intendants. Despite their great financial dependence, they can always appeal to artistic freedom as anchored in the Federal German constitution.

The destruction resulting from the Second World War brought about the second important turning-point. Over seventy theatre buildings were affected in the area comprising the Federal Republic of Germany and West Berlin. Over a hundred theatres have been newly built or restored since that time.

At the start of the 1980s, the 85 city and state theatres in the Federal Republic, which give performances on some 200 stages, receive subsidies totalling 1.3 milliard DM from local authorities and the *Laender*. None of them could exist without such support, which permits high artistic aspirations and largely serves to meet enormous and increasing personnel costs. The money audiences pay for their tickets covers only between 15 and 20 per cent of expenditure.

Impressive achievements in the building and restoration of German theatres after the Second World War were accompanied by revival of a tradition that had declined two hundred years previously with the domestication of the dramatic arts. In the 17th and 18th centuries it was mainly travelling players who brought theatre to the people. They performed on rapidly erected stages, in market squares, or festive meadows. They often had to improvise, and avoided subjecting themselves to a restricted space or strictly established texts.

Such travelling players are brought back to mind by today's endeavours to regain for the theatre some of the mobility it has lost, and to free it from being tied to written drama. These include experiments made by many companies in taking flexible and usually smaller-scale productions out of the theatre and into satellite towns, youth centres and homes for old people, and into pubs or prisons where they perform in front of a public that would normally not go to a play.

That was accompanied in the late 1960s by the rise of Free Theatre Groups, theatre collectives and travelling troupes of a markedly contemporary character. Their programme was apparent in their (often untranslatable) names such as Munich's "Kollektiv Rote Rübe"("Beetroot Collective"), West Berlin's "Rote Grütze" ("Red Heads"), and the "Kulturkooperative Ruhr" ("Ruhr Cultural Co-operative"). Their initiators and members often came together for concrete political reasons so as to put across their ideas, whether moral or ideological, on streets and squares and in all kinds of places. They have in common an antipathy towards the orderly and highly administered apparatuses of the bigger theatres.

The touring companies (the most famous in the Federal Republic, "Der grüne Wagen", in fact comes from Switzerland) and the rural theatres *(Landesbühnen)* which receive high subsidies for giving guest performances in the provinces, provide drama on a commercial basis across the country – travelling enterprises moving around in buses, and earning quite well in the process. They are nevertheless dependent on popular plays and stars capable of drawing in the public. That means though that, apart from the 75 places with their own company, there are three hundred other towns in the Federal Republic of Germany where there are regular theatre performances.

Theatres in the Federal Republic at present attract an attendance of around 27 million per year, leaving out of account the many amateur companies and flourishing festivals. Of this total four million are accounted for by touring companies and the many private ensembles, big and small, devoted to the experimental and to unproblematic light entertainment, and existing without any or only a small subsidy.

The federal system in West Germany after the Second World War favoured an extension of competition for the accolade of being the leading theatre metropolis. It was not only cities with over a million inhabitants – West Berlin, Munich, Hamburg, and Cologne – that were involved. Such theatre towns as Frankfurt and Stuttgart, Ulm and Bochum, Kassel, Düsseldorf, and Bremen also made their way to the top.

The status and the aesthetic significance of the Bayreuth Festivals, exclusively devoted to the works of their founder, Richard Wagner's music dramas, have persisted to the present day. Under the direction of Wieland (d. 1966) and Wolfgang Wagner, the composer's two grandsons, the Festival's style has twice been fundamentally changed though. This first happened in the 1950s and 1960s under the dominant influence of producer Wieland Wagner whose symbolism put an end to traditional and theatrically bombastic forms of presentation, and entered the history of opera as the "New Bayreuth style". Bayreuth productions in the 1970s once again became fantastic, historically-oriented, or fairy-tale-like. The production of the "Ring" cycle by Patrice Chéreau, the young French producer, with Pierre Boulez as conductor, marking the hundredth anniversary of the Bayreuth Festival in 1976, attracted particularly much attention.

Bayreuth represents the classical type of bourgeois festival, which has nevertheless brought its contents up to date and made itself more socially accessible. In Recklinghausen in the Ruhr, an attempt was made after the Second World War to establish new traditions. The Ruhr Festival received financial support from the German Trade Union Confederation, developing out of the miners' solidarity with "their" theatre whose continued existence they had helped secure during the difficult time of the immediate post-war years with donations of coal. The festival's slogan of "Art for coal" expresses the actors' debt of gratitude, and is also intended to stress the social obligations of the arts. Over the years though it has become apparent that the concept of a festival aiming at presenting topical productions, modern plays, and exhibitions of contemporary art to a public of workers requires intensified backing from on-going and broad-based cultural activities if it is to retain credibility.

If one surveys the repertoires of three decades of theatre in the Federal Republic of Germany, certain phases become apparent, developments and radical changes. After the chaos resulting from Nazi rule and the world war, there was a surprisingly great wish for theatre. Theatres big and small shot out of the ground like mushrooms. For a time there were theatre performances on two hundred stages in West Berlin alone – in ruins, backyards, and old cinemas. And it was not just a hope of diversion and relaxation that found expression there.

During the 1948/49 season, the first after the currency reform when circumstances started to become more stable again, there was one play in particular that was concerned with resistance and acts of sabotage under the Third Reich – Carl Zuckmayer's "The Devil's General". 53 theatres together accounted for a total of over two thousand performances in that season. At the same time 22 theatres presented Goethe's "Faust", and plays by Shakespeare were shown in no fewer than 78 different productions.

A strong impact was exerted by Wolfgang Borchert's late-expressionist drama about a man returning home, "The Man outside", even though this impact may not have been reflected in numbers of performances. It is also interesting that a classic "post-war drama", Lessing's "Minna von Barnhelm", has remained one of the most frequently performed of plays up to the present day. The world of operetta is headed by Johann Strauß's "Fledermaus" and "The Gypsy Baron", Franz Lehar with the "Merry Widow" and "The Land of Smiles", and Emmerich Kalman with "Countess Maritza" and the "Csardas Princess". Gradually though the musical supplanted the old favourites, and the operetta made way for "My Fair Lady", "Fireworks", "Kiss me, Kate", and "Fiddler on the Roof".

There were hardly any changes in the opera though as far as the choice of works was concerned. The emphasis has been on the standard repertoire, which largely derives from the late 18th and the 19th centuries. Verdi, Mozart, Puccini, Wagner, and Lortzing were more frequently performed than Richard Strauß, and considerably more so than such moderns as Alban Berg, Hindemith, Henze, and Gottfried von Einem. Contemporary music theatre has only very seldom found a lasting place in repertoires despite a large number of premières and a number of works commissioned by the big opera houses.

Change has, however, entered Federal German opera houses from another direction. Celebrated theatre producers – including Hans Neuenfels and Hansgünther Heyme, Rudolf Noelte and Hans Hollmann, Luc Bondy, Jürgen Flimm, and Klaus Michael Grüber – have brought theatrical imagination and experimental bravura into the opera and into works that long had the reputation of being nothing but delicious museum-pieces. This is proving successful too. Younger people's interest in this form of theatre is on the increase.

After the years of facing up to the past in the theatre, there was a vogue for more poetic or philosophical plays from France and England. Jean Paul Sartre, Albert Camus, Jean Anouilh, Jean Giraudoux, George Bernard Shaw, T.S. Eliot, and Christopher Fry were the main authors until Max Frisch and Friedrich Dürrenmatt made their way alongside Carl Zuckmayer as contemporary German-speaking dramatists. The Theatre of the Absurd started to flourish in the 1950s with the arrival of plays by Eugène Ionesco and, even more so, Samuel Beckett, long testifying to perplexity and resignation. Beckett's antipode, Bertolt Brecht, was initially faced with narrow-minded political resistance in the Federal Republic of Germany but received full acceptance after 1960. His didactic plays became a theatrical yardstick in the following decade.

A sensation was provided in 1963 by Rolf Hochhuth's "Representative", a denunciation of the Pope's role during the Nazi persecution of Jews. This was followed by further documentary plays – Heinar Kipphardt's "In der Sache J. Robert Oppenheimer", "Vietnam-Diskurs" and "The Investigation" by Peter Weiss, Tankred Dorst's "Toller", and Hochhuth's "Soldiers". These plays were influenced by Erwin Piscator, the politically-oriented man of the theatre, and played their part in the politisation of the Federal German theatre, being clearly affected at the end of the Sixties by the activities of revolutionary students. For a short time the theatre seemed to lose its function as "temple of the muses", preserver of tradition, and as an institution of bourgeois self-satisfaction, and it also lost much of its public.

Those years when the theatre also went onto the streets with the students and art as a value per se was subordinated to higher evaluation of political objectives were, however, followed by a decade of withdrawal, new sensibilisation, and self-reflection on the stage. Peter Handke had in 1966 written a celebrated "Publikumsbeschimpfung" ("Attack on the public") but in 1973 there appeared a play of his – with the title of "Die Unvernünftigen sterben aus" ("They are dying out") – which recommended showing understanding even for the feelings of capitalists. Political programmes and agitprop again largely gave way to depiction of human scruples, contradictions, unpredictability, and often also doubts about the dramatic arts' capacity to bring about change.

At the same time, new and younger German authors made their appearance, critical realists such as Wolfgang Bauer, Harald Sommer, and Peter Turrini, who mainly emphasised the artificiality of our everyday and ideas about art; and Rainer Werner Fassbinder, Martin

Sperr, and, above all, Franz Xaver Kroetz, who invoked the long-forgotten dramas of Marieluise Fleißer, a pupil of Brecht's, depicting unimportant people in difficult situations, and calling for the showing of sympathy. The people's theatre of Horvath and O'Casey also gradually made its way.

Alongside all that, Gerlind Reinshagen and Thomas Bernhard, an Austrian much-performed in the Federal Republic of Germany, wrote and still write tragi-comedies concerned with human weakness, illness, death, and courage. Plays dealing with historical parallels and the current social situation have become rarer since Dieter Forte's bold treatment of "Martin Luther & Thomas Münzer" (1971).

Botho Strauß constitutes an exception in the contemporary theatre. No-one else gives such significant expression to the change of mood that has been viewed in recent years as a turning-point in the Federal Republic and elsewhere. Strauß (b. 1944) played a forthright part in the Sixties as a theatre critic, and then went as dramaturg to Peter Stein's Schaubühne in West Berlin, helping shape and further develop what was certainly the most influential German theatre company of the early Seventies. He has also written plays which increasingly became the most sensitive depictions of contemporary realities, showing individual longings in their threatening anonymity. Such plays as "Bekannte Gesichter, gemischte Gefühle", "Trilogie des Wiedersehens", and "Groß und klein" approach extremely closely to the present day.

Powerful and celebrated producers are also of great importance for theatre in the Federal Republic of Germany, sometimes displacing interest in young authors. They mainly stick to the classics, like their fellows at the opera. In recent years, these new and often unusual attempts at approaching the classics have led to what were perhaps the aesthetically most attractive and often most exciting productions. These included Peter Zadek's stagings of Shakespeare and Ibsen, and Claus Peymann's interpretations of Goethe, Schiller, and Kleist. Peter Stein should be mentioned again in this connection alongside Rudolf Noelte, Peter Palitzsch as upholder of the succession to Brecht, Niels-Peter Rudolph, Alfred Kirchner, and Ernst Wendt. They, and many others, have long filled the gaps created by the death of such great producers as Jürgen Fehling, Heinz Hilpert, Gustaf Gründgens, and Fritz Kortner. Director's theatre has become a catch-phrase. Only recently has sufficient recognition been again accorded to the fact that theatrical quality is largely dependent on the quality of the actors.

The "shop-window" of German-speaking theatre, the annual Theatre Encounter in West Berlin to which a jury invites its selection of the season's most important productions, reflected this trend towards director's theatre in the 1970s, which was one reason why a crisis developed. Director's theatre as the spoilt child of the theatre critics who were over-represented in the jury – is theatre-makers' criticism of the Theatre Encounter, whose continued existence can only be assured by way of reforms. The first step in this direction was the inclusion at the 1980 Theatre Encounter of a "play market" where well-known actors read from still unpublished plays by famous and unknown authors. The Mülheim Theatre Days, which have been devoted since 1976 to the premières of new works, also re-emphasised the fact that plays have to be written before they can be given a first performance. The 10,000 DM Mülheim Dramatists Prize has gone to such people as Franz Xaver Kroetz, Gerlind Reinshagen, and Martin Sperr.

Theatre for children and young people has become of great importance in recent years. The fairy-tale tradition has been slowly shaken off, and adventurous subject-matter from our own age is being discovered and performed alongside emancipatory and educational activities as practiced in exemplary fashion by the West Berlin "Grips" ensemble.

The vitality of theatre in this country is thus also demonstrated in increasing readiness to perform for the youngest of audiences, providing a counterweight to the wonderful theatrical happenings that the adult public can so often experience with modern dramatists and still often enough with the classics.

Dietmar N. Schmidt

Foyer of the Bonn City Theatre.

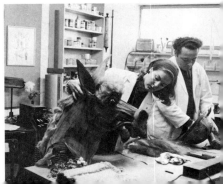

Behind the scenes at Bonn's City Theatre: the wig-making section, putting up sets, and the art workshop.

Claus Peymann gained a great reputation for Stuttgart during his years at the Württemberg State Theatre. His production of both parts of Goethe's "Faust" remains in the memory. The photo shows a detail from the Witches Sabbath in Part II.

Producer Peter Zadek (b. 1926) is known for spectacular staging. As Intendant at the Bochum Theatre (1972–75) he presented an extensive Shakespeare cycle. From l. to r.: Ulrich Wildgruber as Hamlet, Eva Mattes as Gertrude, and Hermann Lause as Claudius.

Producer Peter Stein has made his mark on the Schaubühne am Halleschen Ufer in West Berlin for years now. The photo shows a scene from Maxim Gorky's "Summer Folk".

Theatre in the Federal Republic often has dramatist Franz Xaver Kroetz to thank for controversial productions. The photo shows a Wuppertal staging of "Agnes Bernauer", produced by Andreas Gerstenberg.

The rediscovery of theatre for children and young people, no longer limited to fairy-tale subject-matter, is one of the most important developments in Federal German theatre. The photo shows a scene from "Papadakis", a production by the "Grips" children's theatre dealing with the difficulties of social integration facing Greek workers in West Berlin.

The impetus for emancipatory children's theatre in the 1970s may have mainly come from the fringe but it has now also been taken up by the subsidised theatre. One of the most frequently performed pieces is Friedrich Karl Waechter's "School with Clowns", here in a production by the Frankfurt Theatre.

Marieluise Fleißer (1901–1974) – after years of neglect, her plays in the 1960s became a model for a new generation of young dramatists.

Peter Stein (b. 1937) got going as assistant to Fritz Kortner at the Munich Studio Theatre. Since 1970 he has been a producer – and also manager (up to 1975) – at the West Berlin Schaubühne am Halleschen Ufer.

Rudolf Noelte attempts in his productions to present realistic and humane theatre. His staging of Henrik Ibsen's "The Wild Duck" at West Berlin's Freie Volksbühne was highly regarded.

Cornelia Froboess as Minna von Barnhelm, Munich Studio Theatre, 1976. Dieter Dorn's restrained and faithful production amounted to rediscovery of Lessing's classical comedy.

The International Free Theatre Festival was held in Munich's Olympic Park in 1979. Around a thousand performers from all over the world offered over a hundred programmes during these two weeks.

The Ruhr Festival, under the auspices of the German Trade Union Confederation and the city of Recklinghausen (North Rhine-Westphalia), is the high-point of trade union cultural activities. For eight weeks in the year, the Festival Theatre in Recklinghausen becomes a place for encounters between artists and workers. The photo shows a scene from a festival production of "Lysistrata" (Producer: Heinz Engels).

The Bad Hersfeld Festival in Hesse has been held in the monastery ruins every year since 1951. 37,400 people attended the 1979 festival productions (July 3 to August 5) and 12,000 accompanying events. The photo shows an open-air performance.

In 1978 the Federation of German Amateur Theatres linked 459 companies with an associated membership of 25,003 people. The organisation is mainly concerned with providing training and support for lay actors and their organisations so as to raise levels of performance in German amateur theatre, which is a crucial element in cultural life. The photo shows an open-air performance at Bonn by the Chiemgau Folk Theatre.

Among the most attractive curiosities in Federal German theatre are the Kiefersfeld Knights Plays, which include the bloodthirsty romances by Josef Schmalz (1793–1845), the "Peasant Shakespeare".

Ballet has very much increased in popularity in the Federal Republic since the 1960s. The photo shows a scene from Hans Werner Henze's "Orpheus" (with choreography by William Forsythe) at Stuttgart in 1979. Henze (b. 1926), who sees himself as a socialist artist, presented Orpheus as champion of a more humane society in his much-admired new interpretation of the classical myth.

One of the most radical experiments was undertaken by Pina Bausch, the Wuppertal choreographer. Her title, "He takes her by the hand and leads her into the castle. The others follow", (a stage direction from "Macbeth") is all that is left of the original in this meditation on the subjective experience of the impossibility of performing Shakespeare.

John Neumeier (above) came from John Cranko's Stuttgart ballet, and today, as director of the ballet at the Hamburg State Opera, is viewed as being the most outstanding choreographer in the Federal Republic.

The "Triadic Ballet", for which Oskar Schlemmer, the Bauhaus artist, devised choreography and costumes in 1922, was reconstructed by Gerhard Bohner in 1977, and performed at West Berlin, Stuttgart, and Munich. The photo shows Colleen Scott and Ivan Liska of the Bavarian State Opera.

A three-tiered simultaneous scene from Götz Friedrich's 1976 Hamburg staging of "The Soldiers" by Bernd Alois Zimmermann (1918–1970). This opera, based on J.M.R. Lenz's Sturm und Drang drama, was premièred in 1965, and became one of the few works of contemporary music theatre to be taken up in the repertoire.

Emperor Wilhelm II encounters Geno-
veva, the white fawn – a scene from an
ironical musical setting of a trivial late
19th century play by Detlef Müller-Siemens, then 21 and a pupil of Ligeti's.
This composition was commissioned by
Second German Television in 1978.

Johann Wolfgang von Goethe's "Torquato Tasso" was impressively staged by
Claus Peymann at Bochum in 1980.

The Munich National Theatre, home of the Bavarian State Opera, during the July 1979 Opera Festival. This classical building by Karl von Fischer was completely destroyed during the Second World War and re-opened in 1963. During the regency of Ludwig II, an enthusiastic Wagnerian, "Tristan und Isolde" and "Die Meistersinger von Nürnberg" received their premières here.

Jean Cox, the American tenor, in the third act of "Siegfried" in 1974. The bare set ▶ for Wolfgang Wagner's production (which has now been succeeded by a more recent staging) is characteristic of the abstract "New Bayreuth style" with which Wieland Wagner initiated the cleansing of the Festival in 1951.

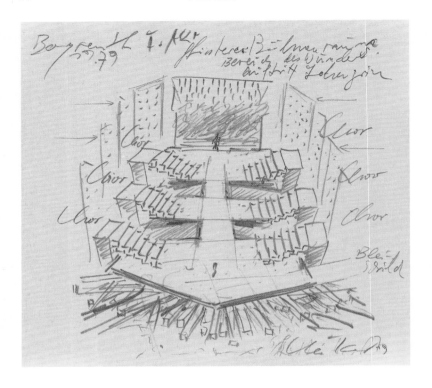

The Bayreuth Festival was established by Richard Wagner in 1876, and became the fateful scene of German chauvinism under the Third Reich. After the Second World War this place of pilgrimage was transformed into a workshop under the direction of Wagner's grandsons, Wieland (1917–1966) and Wolfgang (b. 1910). Among the most controversial and daring productions of recent years were Patrice Chéreau's 1976 "Ring" cycle (the first Bayreuth production to be filmed for television without any cuts in its fifteen hours) and Götz Friedrich's 1979 "Lohengrin". Here a scene from "Lohengrin" with Karin Armstrong and Peter Hoffmann in their bridal garments, and a stage design by Günther Uecker (b. 1930), the German painter and object artist.

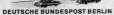

Music

Music, in accordance with its essence as the 'art of sound', as tonal events, is not bound by linguistic frontiers. That explains the fact that German music was always a part of the overall developments in Europe, and can only with difficulty be considered apart from the reciprocal impact of stimulus and influence. On the other hand, the people who made music – composers, interpreters, and even the accompanying listeners – were in a situation of dependence with regard to highly nationalistic social conditions and historical constellations. That frequently impeded free and unprejudiced exchanges, particularly in times of great self-importance among European states, and in general resulted in an astonishing delay in implementation of that idea of understanding among peoples which seems to be implicit in music. This delay lasted almost until the middle of our century.

There had in fact been signs in earlier epochs of musical "frontier-crossing" without regard for origins and nationality. Ludwig van Beethoven from the Rhineland and Johannes Brahms from Hamburg lived and worked in Vienna during their most important creative periods. Franz Liszt, born in Hungary, came to Weimar and even established a "New German School" there. Arnold Schoenberg, leader of the "Viennese School", received a call to Berlin in 1925, succeeding Ferruccio Busoni, a German-Italian, in responsibility for a Master Class, with Franz Schreker, the Academy director from Vienna, as a colleague. These periods of freedom of movement were, however, flanked by times of chauvinistic rigidity. The terrible experiences of the Second World War were probably needed to make a younger generation, faced with the hopeful task of making a fresh start after 1945, fully aware of the necessity of solidarity and understanding.

The most important centre for this shared fresh start was, rather surprisingly, in the country that had been most deeply affected by the ravages of nationalism. The "International Vacation Courses for New

Music" at Darmstadt/Hesse in the Federal Republic of Germany involved a musically acceptable start towards a doubly de-romanticised future. The confrontation with a changed reality demanded a final leavetaking of the music of the day before yesterday, from a post-romanticism that had still been able to survive in Germany under the backward-looking cultural policy of the National Socialists.

This once mighty tradition came to an end in 1949 with the death of Richard Strauss (b. 1864) and Hans Pfitzner (b. 1869). The re-establishment of links with the vehement, anti-emotional German music of the 1920s, with Paul Hindemith's (1895–1963) neo-baroque objective style, also gradually came to seem impossible to such young German composers as Bernd Alois Zimmermann (1918–1970) or the meteorically successful Hans Werner Henze (b. 1926) as a result of lively discussions with contemporaries from Italy (Bruno Maderna, Luigi Nono, and later Luciano Berio), France (Pierre Boulez), or England (Peter Racine Fricker). Even older composers, who taught or had works performed at Darmstadt and were still to some extent influenced by the Hindemith style, underwent a phase of unreserved rethinking of their positions – as happened with Wolfgang Fortner (b. 1907), Boris Blacher (1903–1975), and Karl Amadeus Hartmann (1905–1963) who came to life again after a period of total inner emigration.

Karlheinz Stockhausen (b. 1928) soon became prominent as an inventive source of stimuli in the search for acceptable and logical compositional procedures which derived their impulse from Anton Webern's structural stringency rather than from Schoenberg's twelve-tone methods. Since he was sufficiently flexible, fearless, and consequential to accept and put to his own purposes the challenges of the next few years – whether it was a question of newly-discovered electronic sounds, the anarchistic ideas of John Cage from America, the incorporation of space in performance, improvisation, or the idea of "world music" – Stockhausen became (together with Henze in his very different way) one of the most internationally celebrated of composers and promoters of contemporary German music. The only possibilities still open to others were either dependence and a gradual process of liberation, as was the case even with Mauricio Kagel (born at Buenos Aires in 1931) and György Ligeti (born in 1923 in Hungary) whose activities are completely based in the Federal Republic of Germany – or a characteristic anti-attitude as is to be found in Helmut Lachenmann (b. 1935), Hans Joachim Hespos (b. 1938), or Wilhelm Killmayer (b. 1927). It is only the most recent generation, the thirty year-olds – Wolfgang Rihm, Manfred Trojahn, Ulrich Stranz,

Wolfgang von Schweinitz, Hans-Jürgen von Bose, and Detlev Müller-Siemens –, who once again accept tonality, tradition, love of extended forms, and large numbers of performers, and have made their way as a result of group solidarity.

A similar breakaway movement, sparked off by different circumstances and with different objectives, has occurred in German jazz in recent years. Dependence on the once predominant and certainly stylistically influential American models was gradually overcome as Europeans gained a new confidence in themselves. The decisive factor there was once again the decision to unite as a group, as a collective for improvisation formed from people with an equal say. The old model, favoured in the USA, of the individual star and "his" combo, which Klaus Doldinger, the saxophonist (b. 1936), largely follows, or the latently competitive nature of choruses, were superseded by a new style based on a sense of things in common, which exerted a direct impact on the music. This "open" jazz, "The new thing", simultaneously operates on several levels. Each player contributes his expressive talent, his virtuosity, his tonal imagination, and his capacity for combination and readiness for understanding.

"The liberation of the individual within the ties of playing together and the emancipation of instruments on the basis of equality of partners explain our re-active playing" (Gunter Hampel, vibraphonist, b. 1937). The most talented German jazz musicians – Albert Mangelsdorff (Trombonist, b. 1928), Manfred Schoof (Trumpeter, b. 1936), Alexander von Schlippenbach (Pianist, b. 1938), Peter Brötzmann (Saxophonist, b. 1941), and others came together to form "Globe Unity". Some of these musicians – always, highly characteristically, in conjunction with non-Germans – teamed up with Wolfgang Dauner (Pianist, b. 1935) and Volker Kriegel (Guitarist, b. 1943) to form the intentionally colourful but less experimental "United Jazz & Rock Ensemble", which as a "Bandleaders' Band" dedicated itself to the principle of increased impact through voluntary union.

It goes without saying that the significance and number of such formations remains limited even within the Federal Republic in comparison with the dominance of the Americans – as can be seen from the programmes at West Berlin's Jazz Festivals and other big events. Apart from the purely quantitative reasons for that there are also valid historical and sociological factors involved. These are intensified to an even greater extent in the spheres of Rock and Pop, and of Songs and Musicals. All the same, "German Kraut Rock" has succeeded in attracting an unexpected amount of international attention. Groups like the aggressive and machine-like "Kraftwerk" (from 1970), the arresting and somewhat eccentric "Scorpions" (from 1968), "Kraan" from West Berlin (from 1971, and now split up), "Hölderlin" in the Rhineland (from 1971), and "Novalis" in Hamburg (from 1972) were able to sing and play themselves free from the sphere of relativising comparisons.

Udo Lindenberg (b. 1946) has relied on a kind of impassioned show-style nonchalence, and the group of musicians calling themselves "Tangerine Dream" (from 1967) have deployed a wide range of electronics in their seduction by sound. Synthesizers, electric versions of traditional instruments, feedback, amplification, and loudspeakers play an essential part in producing the sound experience expected by the listener. It is perhaps for that very reason that song-makers' simpler forms of presentation have gained a special chance as a counter-movement to mechanical embellishment and dazzling lighting. That takes in a broad spectrum of styles including the punk of Nina Hagen (b. 1955), the verbally dextrous liveliness of Reinhard Mey (b. 1942), and the social commitment of Konstantin Wecker (b. 1947) from Bavaria. Commercialism and provinciality largely continue to predominate among Pop and light music. More recent developments and types of playing cannot be transplanted – as is most strikingly clear in the case of the musical.

Two of the most positive characteristics of German musical life – its stability and its socially-founded diversity constantly finding regeneration in tradition – have acted there as an impediment. Pre-established structures are to be found on all sides. Even before people ventured in the early years after 1945 to plan a musical future in changed circumstances, the previously existing framework re-established itself in a number of ways. There was an initial lack, as a result of the destruction of war, of theatres, concert halls, training institutes, and so on, but the most immediate necessities of life had hardly been procured when the *Laender,* local authorities, and private backers began to implement – in the shape of plans at any rate - their architectural ideas about music and the presentation of music.

Once again there arose proscenium-arch theatres with tiers of boxes and balconies alongside handkerchief-shaped concert halls. Only the technical facilities on and behind the stage, the building materials, the colours, and the formal decor were modernised in accordance with the times. Nowhere – with very few exceptions such as Scharoun's circular terracing in West Berlin's *Philharmonie* – was the chance taken of following a fundamentally new concept taking account of different social circumstances or new acoustic findings. Instead historic buildings were in many places lovingly reconstructed.

These restorative elements in musical life in the Federal Republic of Germany are explicable in terms of this firmly established tradition, and that also explains the still astonishing number of publicly subsidised establishments. Of the 68 cities with populations of over 100,000 only 17 – mostly in extensive connurbations – have no orchestra of their own. The distribution of the 100 or so German orchestras also takes in a number of smaller towns, and results in larger places in impressively concentrated activity with, for instance, seven orchestras in Munich alone. Over half of these hundred orchestras also work in theatres or play exclusively in opera houses. 13 other orchestras are attached to a radio station (or play for television), and thus have an impact far beyond the immediate locality. The great expenditure on "saturation" cultivation of concerts and opera – to which must be added an equally extensive infrastructure of centres for musical training – has led to the flourishing of German musical life and frequent exchanges across the national frontiers.

Top orchestras such as the Berlin Philharmonic or the eight Radio Symphony Orchestras have a high reputation for their active cultivation of music and vital playing, carried to all five continents in the course of world tours. The many festivals, the high-points on the German musical scene during the summer months, are a great attraction for many visitors from near and far. The Richard Wagner Festival in Bayreuth provides the most all-embracing and direct confrontation anywhere with this composer's music-dramas. Festivals are also centred around Mozart in Würzburg, Beethoven in Bonn, and Handel in Göttingen. Opera is the main attraction at Wiesbaden and Munich, the organ at Nuremberg, Jazz in West Berlin, and New Music in Donaueschingen. Even Ludwigsburg, Hitzacker, Schwetzingen, Brunswick, Witten, and the Elmau have their own music festivals – so far-reaching is the pleasure in local variants on the harmonious correspondence of place, people, and sound.

The worries of people with responsibility for musical life about a lack of young musicians almost seem unjustified in the face of this picture. This really is a problem though, and for years now the German Music Council, supported by the federal, regional, and local authorities, has taken two forms of effective counter-measures. Early recognition of talent and amateur music-making have been promoted by way of the "Young Music-Makers" competition. A programme for mediating concert engagements for outstanding soloists during their final phase of training between finishing at Conservatoire and starting on a concert career, known as "Federal Concerts by Young Artists" has been established, and also provided the best method of selective scholarships for further studies and attendance at master classes. There is now also a German Music Competition whose prizes are intended to stimulate levels of achievement providing a hope of success in the International Competition organised at Munich by the Federal German Radio Stations.

Extensive development of a network of music schools, to which the German Music Council has devoted particular attention since the 1960s, provides an intermediate sphere between careful surveys of talent among the young and assistance for the highly talented when they start on their careers. These music schools served on the one hand to compensate for reductions in the teaching of music at school, and on the other they filled a need somewhere between love of music and pre-forms of vocational training. There thus developed a more refined graduated scale extending from an initial spontaneous impulse towards music-making to the highest degrees of perfection of a professional musician – without any excluding intermediate transitions but accompanied by mounting demands on sources of public money. The training assistance accorded thus becomes a pre-form of subsidised culture.

Such subsidised culture, however, absorbs – as an efficient system – much of the unrestrained lay impulses at the lower levels the more the culture becomes institutionalised at the highest level. The constraints of a movement start to develop. Who can deny that the stabilising subsidised culture in many cases becomes an obstacle for the unusual? Active promotion of New Music is gladly pushed aside to the alibi area of special events, and an operatic première such as the "Lear" by Aribert Reimann (b. 1936), which, surprisingly, opened the Munich Opera Festival, was a rare exception there. It is for that very reason that the hardening of representative culture has led recently to an active counter-movement of spontaneous music-making on public squares and streets, in pedestrian zones and underground stations.

Amateur music-making – otherwise only to be found in choral societies, brass bands, or at home – is spreading. It is also certainly to be welcomed when serious composers seek to meet such needs with demanding exercises in sound, utilising materials free of preconditions such as the voice and everyday articles, as Dieter Schnebel (b. 1930) has done, differing there from Carl Orff (b. 1895) whose Pedagogic Music ("Schulwerk") long ago provided a simplification of the range of instruments and basis for performance. The fact is that an intact musical life develops out of its foundations, and needs the restorative powers of its substructure.

Götz Wittich

Ludwig van Beethoven (1770–1827) remains unchallenged at the top of the list of performances of what is known as "serious music". The photo from Bonn's Beethoven House shows a historic occasion in 1958 when Pablo Casals, Mieczyslaw Horszowski, and Sandor Vegk (from r. to l.) gave a concert in honour of the greatest German composer in the house where he was born.

The Berlin Philharmonic is viewed as being the leading European orchestra alongside the Vienna Philharmonic. Herbert von Karajan succeeded Wilhelm Furtwängler in 1955 as its conductor-in-chief, and now holds this office "for life".

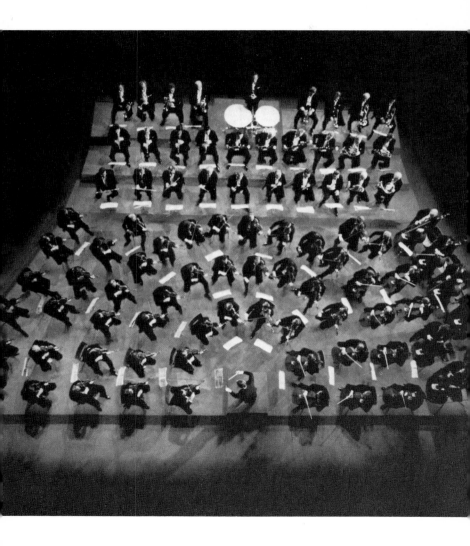

In the summer, culture goes onto the streets in Bonn and in many other places in the Federal Republic. The Austrian pianist Friedrich Gulda used to be an influential interpreter of Beethoven but now he is an advocate of an anarchic "Free Music". The photo shows him improvising at the "Bonn Summer 1979".

Wolfgang Fortner (b. 1907) has utilised twelve-tone and serial techniques in his compositions.

Karl Amadeus Hartmann (1905–1963) was viewed as his epoch's most important symphonist. He also established the Musica viva concerts.

Carl Orff (b. 1895) has helped renew Music Theatre and to establish new forms of musical education.

Boris Blacher (1903–1975) composed music for orchestra, piano, and chamber groups, as well as operas, developing new processes of rhythmic integration.

Karlheinz Stockhausen (b. 1928) is an exponent of electronic music. His compositions include Piano Pieces (1952–56), "Zeitmaße" for five wind instruments, "Kontakte" for electronic sounds, piano, and percussion (1960), "Telemusik" (1966), "Aus den sieben Tagen" (1968), and "Mantra" for two pianos (1970).

Wolfgang von Schweinitz (b. 1953) had a surprising success in 1976 with his opus 12, "Variations on a theme by Mozart".

Karl Richter (b. 1926), organist, conductor, and director of the Munich Bach Choir.

Dietrich Fischer-Dieskau (b. 1925), celebrated for his operatic characterisations and as an interpreter of Lieder.

The Swiss conductor, Sylvia Caduff, musical director at Solingen (North Rhine-Westphalia) is the only woman in such a position in the Federal Republic.

Finding a new use instead of pulling down: an ammunition factory dating from 1850 became a youth centre – "The Factory" in the Altona district of Hamburg. When the building burnt down in 1977, it was decided to rebuild, and that was completed in 1979.

The Essen "Play and Sound Street" where the public could test its skill on simple instruments like tubular bells aimed at presenting music as a source of play rather than culture.

A pop concert in Munich's Olympic Park. The regular open-air events in the summer receive backing from the city's cultural department.

An organ lesson at the Folkwang College in Essen (North Rhine-Westphalia). At present there are sixteen state music colleges in the Federal Republic alongside many urban conservatoires.

Pre-school musical education on what are known as "Orff instruments", which are particularly easy for children to master. Composer and dramatist Carl Orff (b. 1895) developed a musically-founded holistic concept of education, which is today used across the world.

Even in small towns, musical life is not restricted to radio and television. Here pupils at the young people's music school at Ditzingen/Baden-Württemberg (population 12,000) present a serenade for their fellow-citizens.

The organ-builder's activities cover construction, repairs, and tuning of organs and harmoniums. In 1977 there were 197 enterprises in the Federal Republic involved in this craft. The photo shows the cathedral organ at Trier, constructed in 1974 by the Johannes Klais organ workshop from Bonn.

Arts and crafts

Since the turn of the century painters, sculptors, graphic artists, industrial designers, and traditionalist craftsmen have played a crucial part in all spheres of function-oriented art. During the epoch of Art Nouveau the artists who produced designs and the workmen who realised them were seldom one and the same person. In the 1920s, on the other hand, the Bauhaus promoted a new, self-reliant artistic involvement for the craftsman within the concept of artistic unity. The town of Halle's workshops (Burg Giebichenstein) became even more important for that epoch. By the late 1920s "arts and crafts" enjoyed a high reputation. The formal qualities involved did not particularly attract the attention of National Socialism's ideologists of art. Arts and crafts were seldom defamed as being "degenerate", and their tradition remained a vital force even during the years from 1933 to 1945. A number of progressive artists and museum directors even found a zone of safety for the Moderns here and in industrial architecture. After the end of the Second World War, a considerable number of older craftsmen, who had been at work before 1933 and even gained international awards after that, became the teachers of a younger generation. Their political independence had resulted in many of them being harrassed towards the end of the period of Nazi domination – as was Jan Bontjes van Beek, the most important German potter during the first six decades of this century.

Among the traditions providing a basis for further development of arts and crafts in the Federal Republic of Germany was the work of the *Werkbund,* which, after William Morris, had given fresh impetus to the ideas of a new craft-oriented interpretation of art with endeavours towards good industrial design and functional form. The more the *Werkbund* devoted itself to industrial form though, the more arts and crafts seemed to move to the periphery of development. Unease about a degree of monotony in industrial mass production has, however, provided arts and crafts with fresh opportunities in the past ten years.

The highly favourable preconditions also included a turning away from the "handicrafts" of the Art Nouveau epoch and the making of greater distinctions between artistic disciplines. The "artistic craftsman", who pursued all and everything, justly fell a victim to mockery whilst the qualified potter, goldsmith, or artist in glass or textiles became increasingly respected. Reactions to this development were reflected in many public and private collections devoted to just one of these artistic disciplines. Collections of ceramics were the most developed of all, in accordance with the standard achieved, followed by collections of glass and jewellery.

Distinctions between artists corresponded with distinctions between the diversity of crafts. Individualism became the foundation for crafts as well as for painting and sculpture. The pronounced materiality of crafts did not, however, allow development of that intellectualism which predominated within a number of trends in the visual arts in past centuries. In their presentation though the crafts came closer to the liberal arts, and were more and more frequently on show in museums and galleries rather than merely on commercial offer. Ever more comprehensive catalogues appeared, devoted to individuals or groups of craftmen, providing the basis for a growth in informed writing on ceramics, glass, textiles, and goldsmithing.

The more decisively artistic attainment took precedence over fulfilment of functional requirements, the closer crafts came to the liberal arts. The world of "objects", situated in an intermediate sphere between painting and sculpture, made possible a new development in the traditional craft disciplines. It is thus hardly possible any longer today to define crafts as aesthetically convincing utilitarian art. Functional requirements are largely met by industrial production, and German industrial design has excellent achievements to its name, particularly in the sphere of the home and everyday existence, so industrial design has supplanted crafts in many German art school curricula. The consequences involved in this development are not yet clearly apparent since the generation of thirty to fifty-year-old craftsmen and women received their training under the conditions that prevailed until recently. The view that account must be taken of this development is, however, spreading.

Federalism within the cultural and political order in the Federal Republic of Germany also exerts an influence on crafts. Regional bodies are united in the Germans Crafts Association, which organises exhibitions at home and abroad, maintains contact with the international craft organisation, and is active at trade fairs and with publications and public relations. It cannot, however, become as effective as comparable organisations in England and the Scandinavian countries. On the other hand, craftmen's regional activities have eased contact with local publics. Low-membership groupings in the city-states of Hamburg and Bremen have been able to make even more effective use of this advantage than the numerically stronger organisations in *Laender* covering large areas. Crafts receive state assistance by way of awards such as the Hesse State Prize presented annually at the Frankfurt Trade Fair, or the bi-annual Rhineland-Palatinate Ceramics Prize. Some of the available prize money is intended for artists who do not come from the *Land* concerned. North Rhine-Westphalia, Baden-Württemberg, and Hamburg are among the *Laender* that award important prizes of a regional nature, enjoying public esteem.

Despite the regional orientation of cultural policy resulting from the Federal German constitution, there are few regional characteristics in modern German handicrafts. Only where workshops are active within a long-established tradition and have been in the same place for decades, or even centuries, do their products display characteristics linked with a place or a landscape. That only applies today to a number of potteries producing folk art in Franconia, Bavaria, and the Middle Rhine.

Teachers, who were active in a single place for a longer period, have almost never founded a "school" linked with the place concerned. Pupils have almost without exception chosen to live away from the place where they studied, frequently in the countryside around big cities. All kinds of craftsmen are therefore to be found all over the Federal Republic of Germany. The diversity of individual talents cannot easily be ordered in stylistic categories. Only a few aspects and tendencies can be mentioned here as seeming to be particularly characteristic of German handicrafts.

The Bauhaus, the Werkbund, and involvement in industrial design promoted rational, geometrically-oriented developments as in silver-work and ceramics. German ceramics made great use of scientific methods in attainment of an international reputation for glazes. Individualisation promoted the free visual elements that predominate in jewellery, textiles, and glass. Aesthetic and craft criteria are applied strikingly strictly in the Federal Republic of Germany, compared with the situation in the USA or Southern Europe.

The products of modern craftsmanship have in the meantime become a recognised part of museum collections but presentation of such objects remains an unsolved problem in many places. Following the example set by the Museum of Arts and Crafts in Hamburg, Munich, Stuttgart,

Frankfurt, Cologne, and West Berlin will be equipped in the years ahead for adequate presentation of their collections in permanent exhibitions, thus assuring crafts of their status as an independent form of art.

Heinz Spielmann

The Christmas Fair organised by North German craftsmen at Hamburg's Museum of Arts and Crafts every December. This attracts people from England and Scandinavia alongside the 70 German craftsmen and women and a public of around 30,000. This Fair is one of the most important displays of German crafts, and also promotes contacts between artists and the public.

The Bauhaus was set up at Weimar in 1919 by architect Walter Gropius (1883–1969) who combined the art college and the craft school there. Among the teachers at the Bauhaus were Ludwig Mies van der Rohe (1886–1969), Wassily Kandinsky (1866–1944), Lyonel Feininger (1871–1956), Paul Klee (1879–1940), Oskar Schlemmer (1888–1943), and Gerhard Marcks (b. 1889). The Bauhaus was the stylistic power house for all aspects of the modern age.

Today important painters still provide tapestry designs which are then realised by Gobelin manufacturers. "The Magic Flute" by Oskar Kokoschka (1886–1980) was produced by the Munich Gobelin-Manufaktur.

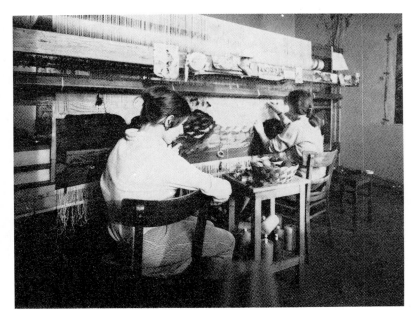

The tradition of weaving can be traced in Germany back to the Middle Ages. Jugendstil around 1900 and the Bauhaus epoch of the 1920s endeavoured to revive this craft, which had gone into decline after the 18th century. The photo shows a loom in the studio of Uta Rösinger-Ohnsorge, Karlsruhe (Baden-Württemberg).

White textile relief by Peter and Ritzi Jakobi, Neubärenthal near Pforzheim, Baden-Württemberg.

Most textile artists produce work based on their own designs. The photo shows Anka Kröhnke from Hamburg in front of her carpet "Diagonal Spectral Structure".

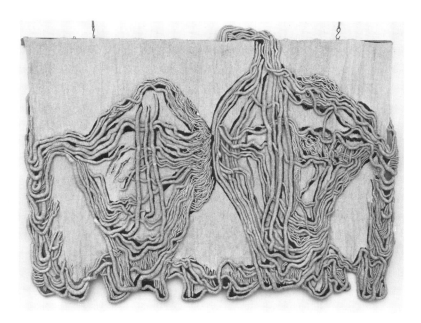

The tradition of artistic construction of musical instruments goes back for centuries in Germany. The main centres are Mittenwald, long celebrated for its violins, in Bavaria, Bubenreuth (also Bavaria), and Trossingen in the Black Forest (Baden-Württemberg). The restoration of old instruments is also viewed as being a part of this craft. The photos show (from above to below): a violin-maker; soldering of a cavalry trumpet (c. 1900) in a workshop of the German Museum in Munich; one of the last master harpmakers, Maximilian Horngacher at Starnberg (Bavaria), constructed the "Orchestra" model shown here; the first rectangular bass recorder is a new development by Paetzold, the Munich instrument-maker.

Wood sculpture and wood-carving are crafts that mainly flourish in Southern Germany. Such high quality sculpture, usually with Christian themes, has been produced there for centuries. Bavarian trade schools in such places as Munich, Garmisch-Partenkirchen, and Oberammergau are well aware of what is involved in continuing this tradition. The crafts of carving and sculpture are, however, also taught at training centres in other wooded areas such as the Rhön and Odenwald regions. The photo was taken at the State Vocational School for Wood Sculpture and Carving at Oberammergau.

The art of carving masks is closely linked with the Alemannic carnival. The photo shows a Black Forest wood-carver in his workshop.

Simple, individually-shaped vases with subtle glazes and sculptural forms are of equal importance in Federal German ceramics. The photos (from above to below) show: Karl Scheid in front of his kiln after firing; stoneware still-life object by Antje Brüggemann, Bad Hersfeld (Hesse); stoneware object by Barbara Stehr, Tornesch (Schleswig-Holstein); stoneware vase by Karl Scheid, Düdelsheim (Hesse); stoneware vase by Jan Bontjes van Beek, Dehme (North Rhine-Westphalia).

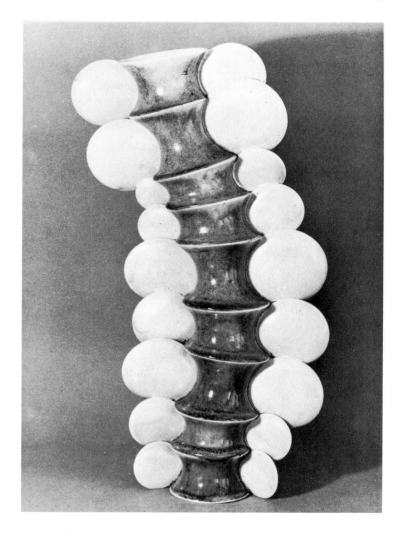

Beate Kühn, "Ear Tower", porcelain, Düdelsheim (Hesse), 1977.

Ursula Scheid, stoneware vessel, Düdelsheim (Hesse), 1980.

Isgard Moje-Wohlgemuth, glass vase, Hamburg, 1979.

Freia Schulze, "Dream", glass container with lid and silver mount, 7 cm in diameter, Groß-Grönau (Schleswig-Holstein).

Willi Pistor, "Object 1", prismatic, polished rectangular element with blue sphere, height 13 cm, Hadamar (Hesse).

Glass-artist Klaus Moje at work, Hamburg 1978.

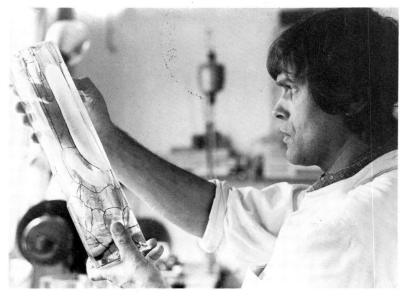

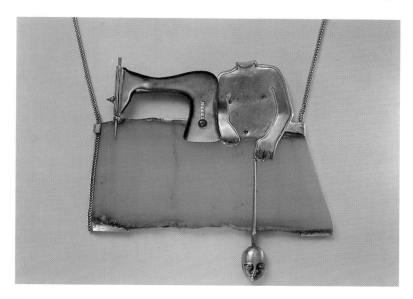

Ulrike Bahrs. Necklace – gold, silver, steel, chrysoprase, mother of pearl, and garnet, Munich 1978.

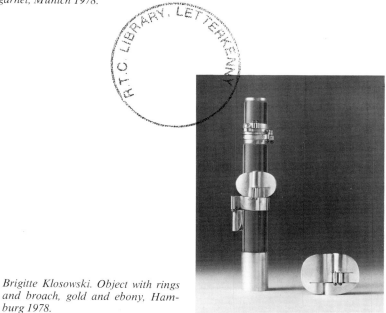

Brigitte Klosowski. Object with rings and broach, gold and ebony, Hamburg 1978.

One of the celebrated examples of 1920s architecture – Bruno Taut's "Uncle Tom's Cabin" settlement at Zehlendorf, part of what is now West Berlin.

Architecture

Modern German architecture had particular difficulty after the Second World War in finding a convincing character of its own since the enormous extent of destruction – with three quarters of some places in ruins – enforced a form of reconstruction where a roof over the head was the most important thing rather than any thought of beauty.

Nazi dictatorship had so effectively cut off the past that no post-war attempt was made to build on progressive elements in German architecture of the 1920s. Once the "Economic Miracle" got under way, architects took their bearings from the "international style" which came from the USA and then Scandinavia to influence new building in the emerging Federal Republic of Germany.

During that period hardly anything was built here with a strength and impact of its own. Characteristic of the time is the collection of unrelated adjacent appartment blocs in West Berlin's "Hansaviertel" (1956), designed by what were then the world's most celebrated architects. These men still believed in the clean-cut residential town amid greenery with high-rise buildings in the park. Urban "accomodation" was not built – instead areas were formally decorated with assemblages of high and low building elements.

In addition, what was technically possible seemed desirable. The "car-oriented town" was not just a conceptual model. It was almost thought natural to subordinate the town to traffic rather than the other way round. The principles of design taken over from America were applied ever more rigidly. Louis Sullivan's celebrated formula of "Form follows function" was taken so literally that soon only function was recognisable in an architecture without any graspable, let alone unmistakable, form.

Architects Hentrich and Petschnigg conceived the Thyssen skyscraper (1960), modern Düsseldorf's landmark, in accordance with the view that technical progress is the main social motor. Cool and elegant, self-assured and yet anonymous, these three slender, staggered buildings of glass diffuse a perfect and clear harmony – architecture without a blemish but also without a soul.

How different is Hans Scharoun's eruptive, contradictory, unfinished, and yet transformative (of music into architecture) work for the Philharmonic Hall (1963) in West Berlin. The roofs have movement, and the facades are like many faces. The auditorium has similarities with a vineyard slope, and the staircases are a spatial adventure. The Philharmonic Hall is an exception though. Only here could Scharoun, the champion of "organic building", realise his vision almost completely. Current trends were moving in another direction.

That direction is characterised by the "Twentieth Century Gallery", the "National Gallery" in West Berlin, close to the Philharmonic Hall. This is a late building by Ludwig Mies van der Rohe – basically only an elegant, black, flat roof, supported by mobilely-articulated slender columns of great technical fascination. The facade is so-to-speak "nothing", immaterial, only glass. The extent to which Mies van der Rohe regarded this modern classical temple of art as a work of art in itself is demonstrated by his contempt for function whereby he banished the actual museum into the cellar so that the purity of his architectural creation would not be muddied by "contents".

This building is also a special case since German architects had in the meantime discovered "Brutalism", and celebrated absolute orgies with sculpturally formed concrete. Hundreds of new churches became more or less successful monuments to a new Expressionism. Whilst this fashion was still going strong, Gottfried Böhm summed it up unmistakably with the town hall (1964) at Bensberg near Cologne. This modern "castle" lies like a crown on the heights of a small town. Movement becomes form. There is no longer any clear principle of organisation, and complicated rhythms replace a regular beat in the structuring and movement of facades and construction units.

At that time too, a perverted form of concrete Brutalism established a bad precedent in house-building. That is why the planners of West Berlin's "Märkisches Viertel" (1965) threw residential mountains sky-high with their jagged silhouettes 22 floors up, lacking, however, any connection with the real needs of the people stowed away there, people who would prefer to live close to the ground and below the tree-tops. The disaster of the Märkisches Viertel brought about a turning-point. People returned to the long despised idea of living around courtyards, and to the spatial impact of streets comprehended from both front and back as in the Steilshoop settlement at Hamburg. Low-rise but dense forms of housing have also made their way again as in Peter Volkamer and Frank Wetzel's Volkárdy Park at Ratingen (1974).

Alongside these general trends there have, time and again, been individual achievements in German architecture, which either sparked off further developments and imitations, or else remained admired exceptions. These include the cylindrical high-rise building Karl Schwanzer devised for BMW at Munich (1972), the joyous tent-like architecture with its swaying roofs over Munich's Olympic Park by Günter Behnisch and Partners (1967/72), Egon Eiermann's offices for Olivetti at Frankfurt (1972), the highly polished prisms of Kraemer, Pfennig, and Sieverts' administrative building for the German Health Insurance Company at Cologne (1970), the integrally conceived "Passerelle" pedestrian zone, half above and half below the earth, at Hanover (1976), the pleasant and functional schools by Günter Behnisch and Partners (Lorch 1973, Dachau 1975, Rothenburg 1979), the artistically successful aspects of Constance's new university (1972), and Ekkehard Fahr's formally and functionally convincing factory at Kaiserslautern (1973).

Peter M. Bode

Conservation of historic monuments

Conservers of historical monuments were faced with almost impossible tasks in the Federal Republic of Germany after the Second World War when the materials they required were hardly available.

Difficult structural work had first to be carried out on almost all the important cathedrals and churches in the battered towns so as to ensure their safety. This was followed by reconstruction and extensive restoration. This opportunity was often utilised for recreation of what was felt to be a more precious earlier state of construction (as in the case of the Romanesque church of St. Michael at Hildesheim in Lower Saxony), or for using modern materials in repairing old styles of building. Ferroconcrete beams replaced what had previously been wooden constructions.

Secular buildings were more frequently subjected to far-reaching restructuring. Changes in need resulted in large-scale replanning of interiors (as at the Hanover Opera) or in the rebuilding in modern styles of elements that had been destroyed (the Germanic National Museum at Nuremberg).

Less attention was in general paid to tradition in the reconstruction of devastated town centres. There are few examples of reconstruction in accordance with what had formerly existed as in the case of the main market place at Münster in Westphalia, or of preservation of a town's original layout with its network of streets and building lines, or of attention being paid to local characteristics (roof shapes and angles, and utilisation of local materials) in the rebuilding of destroyed houses. Mention can only be made here of the reconstruction of the old town of Nuremberg in accordance with a "master plan" approved by the city council in 1950. Most local building and planning authorities instead took the chance to reorganise their urban areas in accordance with modern ideas. Rudolf Hillebrecht's plans for Hanover were thought exemplary at that time.

Today, at the start of the 1980s, the preservation of historic monuments entails a diversity of activities, many of which are new or have been expanded.

Most of the necessary specialists continue, however, to be involved in the "classical" tradition of caring for outstanding monuments. This has long moved beyond merely providing simple protective measures or constant care to keep in check natural forms of wear and tear. What is involved now is the development of modern chemical, physical, and technological means of conservation in the face of accelerated processes of decay caused by intensified air pollution and the vibrations resulting from road and air traffic. Solution of such problems as conservation of stone, consolidation of foundations, and installation of protective screens in front of mediaeval stained-glass windows demands close co-operation between scientists and technicians. A number of specialised institutes have been established or have intensified their work, and have already accumulated extensive experience. These include the Doerner Institute at Munich, the Dr. H. Oidtmann Glass Workshops at Linnich in North Rhine-Westphalia, and the Dr. G. Frenzel Institute for Research into Stained Glass at Nuremberg. A number of *Laender* now have both workshops for the restoration of movable works of art and research facilities of their own. Mention should be made here of the central laboratory for stone conservation, which the Bavarian Land Office has at Seehof Castle near Bamberg.

Site offices are now needed to co-ordinate and carry out a constantly increasing amount of maintenance and restoration work on important cathedrals. The most extensive measures have long been necessary on Cologne cathedral where the replacement of the original crumbling sandstone by more resistant basalt lava almost amounts to gradual reconstruction.

The renovation of important interiors in historic buildings – such as Limburg cathedral in Hesse, and Bamberg cathedral and Pommersfelden Castle in Bavaria – have been among the most expensive and far-reaching of conservation projects in recent decades. Frequent overpainting and extensive changes in earlier times often make it difficult to decide how the interior should look. Attention must be paid to both aesthetic and historical factors.

The restoration of Veit Stoss's "Angelic Greeting" from Nuremberg's Lorenzkirche, carried out during the Dürer anniversary year of 1971, and the restoration of Bernt Notke's "Triumphal Cross" at Lübeck Cathedral in Schleswig-Holstein serve to demonstrate the trail-blazing work done on movable works of art. Decisions about what conservation measures to apply were based on systematic research into the origins and history of these polychrome wooden sculptures. Both operations were carried out in an "ad hoc" workshop under the supervision of an international team of experts.

A new branch of conservation came into being when protection was accorded to technological monuments, and artefacts from the beginnings of "industrial culture" were collected and looked after by special museums. Early utilitarian architecture such as factory halls, water towers, pithead gear, and railway stations are particularly threatened by decay and demolition since their specific function and site make it difficult to adapt them to new production methods or different functions. Many of the once spectacular engineering constructions required for the transport system no longer meet today's demands, and must ultimately be replaced by new constructions on the same site – as will probably be the case in the near future with the Grosshesseloher bridge over the Isar near Munich.

Interdisciplinary co-operation is particularly necessary in the sphere of conservation of urban monuments and of groups of buildings. During the euphoric building programmes of the 1960s, many communities whose historic town centres had survived the war without extensive damage followed modern ideas about rebuilding and renovation. These mainly involved a one-sided concentration on shops, department stores, banks, insurance companies, and public administrations in town centres, which were also opened up for individual forms of transport. The increasingly desolate nature of urban centres was seldom compensated for by extensive pedestrian zones, and finally led to counter-movements, which often originated among the people directly affected by drastic speculative plans for rebuilding.

Preservation of a diversity of functions in urban living areas, taking man as the measure of what is desirable, cannot, however, exclusively be the task of the people involved in the preservation of historic monuments. It must become the concern of the entire community, and as such be taken into account in community planning.

It is not possible or desirable either to apply the same principles of conservation to the preservation of towns as to the restoration of monuments. The emphasis should be on the preservation of character-istic styles and monuments even when it is necessary to replace historical by new buildings. Plans for "town houses" (see the section on "Architec-ture") offer a starting-point in that direction. Reservations seem necess-ary, however, with regard to the methods of "cultivation of townscape" primarily developed in the Anglo-Saxon countries. These frequently merely concentrate on the preservation, or theatrical ordering, of facades behind which the authentic historical substance has long been taken away and replaced by extended buildings whose functional nature perhaps also exerts a destructive influence on the town.

Conservers of monuments and, to an even greater extent, public planners must devote more attention today to the preservation of former workers housing and historic village centres. The restructuring of processes of production and their displacement to other places entail a danger that these monuments to the life, work, and culture of entire segments of the population may be wiped out or changed beyond recognition. Open-air and ethnology museums can only take on selected individual objects, and are hardly capable of documenting the more extensive interrelationships involved inclusive of the links with society and the landscape.

Conservation of historic monuments in the Federal Republic of Germany is the responsibility of the *Laender*. After the Second World War the *Laender* passed new laws, taking into account the expanded scope of such conservation. The Land Conservation Offices or conservators are in charge of such activities. Many towns with important historic buildings also have conservation offices of their own, or else equivalent sections in their planning and building departments or in their museums.

The various aspects of conservation in the Federal Republic of Germany are internationally represented by way of such bodies as the German National Committee for Conservation of Historic Monuments, the German National Committee in the International Council of Monuments and Sites (ICOMOS), and the German UNESCO Commission in Bonn.

The problems and working methods involved are covered in such specialist magazines as "Deutsche Kunst und Denkmalpflege" (published by the Association of Conservationists in the Federal Republic of Germany, based in Kiel), "Maltechnik – Restauro" (Munich), "Das Münster" (Munich-Zürich), "Burgen und Schlösser" (published by the German Castles Association, Braubach/Rhine), "Die alte Stadt – Zeitschrift für Stadtgeschichte, Stadtsoziologie und Denkmalpflege" (Stuttgart), and to a greater extent in recent years in trade papers dealing with architecture and planning.

Ingrid Brock

Linking history and the present-day. The ruins of the Kaiser Wilhelm Memorial Church in West Berlin, built in 1891–95 and badly damaged in the Second World War, were incorporated in the new church (1960–61) by Egon Eiermann.

A modern building in historic surroundings – the German Africa Line's administrative building in the Altona district of Hamburg. Architects: Hentrich & Petschnigg together with Fritz Rafeiner.

Interior architecture in the public sector. A waiting room for passengers at West Berlin's Tegel airport. Architects: von Gerkan-Marg and Partners.

Pedestrian precincts and areas of urban tranquillity. A fountain in front of the Church of Our Lady in Munich. Below: the pedestrian zone of the Neuhauserstraße in Munich. Planning by Bernhard Winkler in conjunction with Friedrich Hahmann.

The Märkisches Viertel in West Berlin was built between 1963 and 1974 in accordance with plans by an international team of architects. The result earned much praise – and criticism.

West Berlin's Deutsche Oper (1961) was designed by F. Bornemann.

One of the most modern office buildings in the Federal Republic is the BMW administration block at Munich. The architect was Karl Schwanzer.

The Munich Olympic Park with the lake, stadium, swimming pool (foreground), and cycling stadium (background). The architects were Günter Behnisch & Partners, Stuttgart.

Above: View from West Berlin's Radio Tower to the new International Congress Centre, which is linked by a bridge to the trade fair site. Below: a hall in the Centre accomodating up to 5,000 people. Architects: Ralf Schüler and Ursulina Schüler-Witte.

The "Mary, Queen of Peace" church at Neviges (North Rhine-Westphalia), a place of pilgrimage. Built from 1965–67 after plans by Gottfried Böhm.

A view of Bensberg (North Rhine-Westphalia) with the new town hall completed in 1967. The new construction incorporated the old, and followed the line of the former castle wall, thus enclosing the old courtyard. Architect: Gottfried Böhm.

Federal Garden Shows have been held for many years, each time at a different place. They offer landscape architects and garden designers an opportunity for useful planning projects close to towns, and create easily reached recreational areas which remain even after the official show is over. The photo shows the 1979 Federal Garden Show at Bonn on the Rhine.

Constance University – forum and student's dining hall. Built 1970–73 after plans by Eugen Schneble and W. von Wolff.

Regensburg (Bavaria). The ensemble of buildings in the 177 hectare old town centre, whose heart was originally a Roman camp, was placed under protection in accordance with the regulations of the Bavarian Law for the Protection of Historic Monuments (December 1975). There are 1050 individual monuments within this area, most of them dating from the town's mediaeval heyday (above). Typical German half-timbered houses, preservation of which is the object of special efforts all over the Federal Republic. The photo (below) shows the village of Freudenberg near Siegen (North Rhine-Westphalia)

Extensive reconstruction and complex measures for ensuring the safety of buildings were necessary in the case of most public monuments that suffered war damage. The photo shows St. Sebaldus in Nuremberg (Bavaria) immediately after World War II (above). In the rebuilding of the old centre of Nuremberg, 80 % of which had been destroyed in air raids, the town regained at least its external appearance as the result of "guidelines" on adherence to the original layout of streets, and to specific types and angles of roofs, in the "Outline Plan" approved by the town council in 1950 (below).

Colourful renovations of facades are an important element in care of townscapes. The photo shows a restored Jugendstil facade at Munich (Bavaria).

The interior of the Lorenzkirche, Nuremberg, with Veit Stoss' "Angelic Greeting", restored to mark the Dürer centenary in 1971. Up to 19 people from the Federal Republic and elsewhere were involved in the restoration of this ten and a half cwt. free-hanging lime-wood sculpture under the general supervision of the Bavarian Office for the Conservation of Historic Monuments.

The disintegration of walls, external frescoes, mediaeval stained-glass windows, etc, is accelerated by increasing air pollution. The photo shows one of the 12th century Five Prophets (Hosea) at Augsburg Cathedral in Bavaria before (l.) and after (r.) restoration by the Nuremberg-based Dr. Frenzel Institute for Research into Stained Glass.

The former monastery church of St. Michael at Hildesheim (Lower Saxony). Above: after destruction in the Second World War. Below: Reconstruction as a return to the pristine state as ascertained by scholars (1960).

Saving technological monuments is a new task for conservationists. It is difficult in many cases to find a new function for utilitarian buildings which have 'served their time'. The machine hall of this Ruhr coal mine, designed in 1902 by B. Möhring, will house part of a Museum of Technology (above). Below: The "Ravensburg Spinning Works" at Bielefeld (North Rhine-Westphalia), built in 1855, now stands empty.

Rolandseck railway station near Bonn. In 1959 the Federal Railway Authority planned to have this unprofitable 19th century station pulled down. Johannes Wasmuth then installed his "Art and Music" enterprise, a symbiosis of art and social work, there, and saved this classic building until sufficient public interest was aroused and the station could be bought, with state aid, in 1969. The original form was maintained during restoration, and extensions also respected the historical design. The one-time station today serves as a centre for the arts and culture.

The fashion photo working for the couturier. A model in front of a picture by the French painter Henri Rousseau (double exposure).

Design

The Anglo-American term "Design" has been established in the Federal Republic of Germany since the early 1960s. Today it entails activity in two spheres: in visual communication (graphic and photographic design) and in product design (industrial design and fashion design). Fashion has been evident since the rise of the middle class in the eighteenth century, and industrial design since the late ninteenth century, but the sphere of visual communication only developed to its present level of complexity in the post-war period under the influence of perceptual psychology and advertising. Graphic and photographic designers are thus no longer faced with tasks in isolations as used to be the case in devising a poster or producing a studio photograph. The emphasis now is on conceiving and implementing comprehensive strategies of visual mediation for commercial, educational, and artistic subject-matter. The team around Otl Aicher demonstrated the outcome (when all goes well) at the 1972 Olympic Games in Munich. All the visual aspects of organisation of the Games – entrance tickets, uniforms, pictogrammes on sign-posts, publications, and details of the opening and closing ceremonies – were designed in accordance with a unified concept, endowing the event with an unmistakable identity, and at the same time pointing to its playlike character. That example also makes clear what distinguishes such "communications design" from traditional functional graphics – the new importance that psychological considerations have assumed alongside purely visual factors. The same can be said of industrial product design whereas makers of fashion are subject to particular market mechanisms despite their great freedom in such details as creating fabrics.

Design serves an important function in the Federal Republic of Germany as in all highly-developed industrial states. Training for designers is provided in study courses taking between six and twelve semesters at Polytechnics (some of which are integrated in Comprehensive Universities) and Academies of Art. The attractive image of jobs involving design has helped make such courses very popular with the result that there is already a surplus of would-be designers on the labour market. The professional organisations looking after the interests of designers include the Federation of German Graphic Designers and the Association of German Industrial Designers, both based in Düsseldorf (North Rhine-Westphalia), and the Federation of Self-Employed Photos at Stuttgart (Baden-Württemberg). The German Craft Federation (Deutscher Werkbund) views itself as a comprehensive forum, available to designers, architects, and crafts-people for discussion of aesthetic and social issues. Standards in production design are the particular concern of four institutes in the Federal Republic which pursue "education through exemplification" by way of exhibitions of exemplary work, discussions, and publications – the Design Council at Darmstadt, the Design Centre at Stuttgart, the International Design Centre at Berlin, and the House of Industrial Design at Essen (now being rebuilt after a fire). The museums of arts and crafts have also long been collectors of modern design.

If, despite such signs of outward success, mention is made here of the necessity of a reorientation of design theory in the Federal Republic in the near future, then this thesis calls for substantiation by way of an historical digression. The history of the concept of design is indivisibly linked in Germany with two institutions, the already-mentioned Deutscher Werkbund (established at the instigation of architect Hermann Muthesius in Munich in 1907, disbanded by the National Socialists in 1933, and revived after the Second World War), and the Weimar Bauhaus launched as an interdisciplinary College of Design by Walter Gropius in 1919, moved to Dessau in 1925, closed in 1933, and re-opened in American exile as the New Bauhaus. The Werkbund may have paved the way for mass-produced industrial products but it was left to Gropius and his colleagues to create the foundations of modern design. The formal criteria thus developed have lost none of their validity up to the present day – remaining true to the material and craft involved, ergonometric design without disregard of aesthetic aspects, and development of form out of function. All these classical demands were, however, developed in Bauhaus theorising out of the social utopianism rooted in the atmosphere of starting something new prevalent in the century's first post-war period, still seeing concrete social hope in modern technology. The 1920s designer had a priori to view the industrial products he was shaping as being meaningful. They embodied the hope of economic recovery, of improvement of the quality of life, an increase in leisure, and even the emancipation of workers and women from their dependent roles in industry and the household.

The resumption of high-quality design in the Federal Republic of Germany after the Second World War carried on the unbroken Bauhaus tradition, and took over its aesthetic practice without rethinking the theory behind it. The unexpectedly rapid economic recovery in the

1950s was linked with a social restoration that was not to be compared with the intellectual climate of the Weimar Republic during the Bauhaus period, which led designers astray into contenting themselves with pragmatic solutions for increasing numbers of tasks. Their endeavours were directed towards "good form", a self-restriction that would have seemed out of question to the artists of the Bauhaus. German design – or at least its peak achievements – certainly attained a worldwide reputation once again. The work of the Ulm College of Design (1955–1972) must receive express mention in this connection. At the same time, German design's characteristic theoretical weakness led to a dependence on industry and advertising where there was a risk of loss of its utopian potential.

The ecological crisis that got under way at the start of the 1960s and seems to be determining the last quarter of the century has made this apodictically sketched outline become particularly apparent. Almost all the technical possibilities envisaged 50 years previously by the founders of the Bauhaus are today reality – but the associated hopes have almost all remained unfulfilled. Making work easier by way of ergonometric design has not infrequently changed into depriving work of meaning.

Rationalisation measures have not only led to more leisure time, killed in front of the TV screen; they have also resulted in industrial unemployment with unforeseeable social and political consequences, and in dependence on suppliers of energy and repair services in the home. We have come up hard against the limits to growth, and we are faced with a vicious circle of economic and technological constraints scarcely controllable any longer, watching helplessly as spaceship earth's energy budget gets out of balance.

Of all the artistic disciplines product design is most directly confronted by this complex of problems. It alone has the possibility of acting rather than just passing comment. Appeal to the intellectual tradition of the Bauhaus means in this context to reject its theory as no longer contemporary. Radical rethinking, also exerting an impact on designers' everyday vocational practise, is all the more urgently necessary in view of the fact that design constitutes modern utilitarian culture per se. Design surrounds the population of industrial states at their every step – and it could be employed for objectives apart from the arousing of consumer wishes. Even within their economic dependence on industry and advertising as the two main sources of work, designers can still be expected to reflect on the possible long-term consequences of their ideas before they set to work. One fewer button to press in a factory, a car, or on a coffee machine is an expensively bought design objective if the ultimate price to be paid consists of modern man's pathological passivity, which social psychologist Erich Fromm recognised as the most severe burden for our future. If this rethinking – which must of course extend to the raw materials and energy required for the objects to be designed – is successful, modern design in the Federal Republic of Germany is today perhaps faced with the greatest upheaval to date within its seventy-year history.

Thomas Piltz

Design studio in a carpet factory.

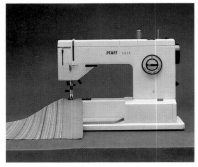

Examples of industrial design. Rosenthal AG at Selb (Bavaria), rocking chair (above l.), and an art object for everyday use – tea-pot ornamented with a design by HAP Grieshaber (below l.). Pfaff AG at Kaiserslautern (Rhineland-Palatinate), household sewing machine (above r.). Braun AG, Frankfurt (Hesse), kitchen equipment (centre r.). Siemens AG at West Berlin and Munich (Bavaria), freely programmable data record (below r.).

A locomotive, series ET 403, of the Federal German Railways.

The Munich Gärtnerplatz Theatre's poster for "The Sleepwalker" won a prize as the best cultural poster for the year 1978.

Posters for the German Federal Railways.

Advertising (incorporating picto-grammes) for Baden-Baden (Baden-Württemberg) as a spa.

Walter Scott's "Quentin Durward" with typography by Juergen Seuss, Niddatal (Hesse).

Textile design is taught in the Federal Republic at two Colleges of Design (Munich and Brunswick), and at Polytechnics and Special Schools (i.e. Fashion Schools). The German Master School of Fashion is at Munich. The photo shows a presentation of some of its creations.

International fashion has been presented at Düsseldorf for over 30 years now. In 1979 more than 1900 exhibitors displayed their collections of women's clothing in the 121st such exhibition.

The "Munich Fashion Week" was first held in March 1960 with 28 firms. Today over 1700 exhibitors from 25 countries present their latest collections to 50,000 buyers in spring and autumn every year. The photo was taken during the 39th Fashion Week in April 1979.

The "Berlin Interchic" is held twice a year in West Berlin. The photo shows a presentation during the autumn 1979 trade fair.

Bernhard Wicki (b. 1919) was an established actor when he changed over in 1958 to direction. He attracted international attention with his anti-war film "The Bridge" (1959).

Film

"The German Filmboom" was how "Newsweek" headed a title story at the beginning of 1976, but success for the German film, which only started to be reflected in box office takings abroad in 1979 with Fassbinder's "The Marriage of Maria Braun" and the great international triumph of Volker Schlöndorff's version of Grass's "Tin Drum", was the outcome of a long development, accompanied by many setbacks and still far from completed. It all started in 1962 with a move towards renewal comparable with the *Nouvelle Vague* in France. "The old film is dead. We believe in the new film" – concluded the *Oberhausen Manifesto,* a declaration issued by young German film-makers during the West German Festival for Short Films. These young directors could, however, only provide confirmation of their faith years later. The inroads made by National Socialism on the art of the film in Germany had been too great. The loss of production facilities, which were in Berlin's Eastern sector after 1945, played a crucial part too. The return of the German film to the international reputation it had had in the 1920s and the start of the Thirties was also hindered though by the general return to traditional values. Film production re-started in West Germany with an insipid farce which had been conceived even before the war was over.

The first facing up to the recent past only occurred in the Federal German cinema in 1947 in such films as Käutner's *In jenen Tagen* or Harald Braun's *Zwischen Gestern und Morgen,* films that were too preoccupied with the private sphere to attain to political analysis. The 1950s were characterised by the predominance of trivial comedies, lachrymose family dramas, and flat "homeland films" with settings ranging from the Upper Bavarian Alps to the Lüneburg Heath. There were, all the same, initial attempts at dealing with national reality in the years of reconstruction as in Rudolf Jugert's *Nachts auf den Strassen* (1951), and at facing up to National Socialism in G.W. Pabst's *The*

Twentieth of July, in Käutner's film of Zuckmayer's *The Devil's General* (1955), and in *As the Devil Came at Night* (1957) by Robert Siodmak who returned for a time from American exile.

The first attempts at renewal were undertaken by loners. In 1959 Bernhard Wicki from Switzerland made his anti-war film *The Bridge* in the Federal Republic of Germany. Two years earlier Ottomar Domnick, a Stuttgart psychiatrist, had worked together with Hans Magnus Enzensberger on depiction of the psychic isolation of modern urban man in his *Jonas,* employing almost avantgarde visual means. Herbert Vesely attracted attention in 1962 with *Das Brot der frühen Jahre* after Heinrich Böll. Despite its social and artistic commitment, the film was almost unanimously rejected by the critics but they did at least discuss it. The real turning-point seemed to be imminent in 1966/67 when a considerable number of debut films reached cinemas. The "new German film" became something tangible. The New German Film Board, brought into existence by the Federal Ministry of the Interior and later financed by the *Laender,* has provided support up to the present day for debut feature films by young directors. In 1966 these included Alexander Kluge who achieved an initial international success with the Venice Festival prize for *Taking Leave of Yesterday.* Kluge was also one of the few directors able to fulfil the Oberhausen Manifesto's promise of developing a new language for the film. In his reflections on contemporary life in our state, as exemplified in a young woman who does not find her way in this society, he linked documentary and fictitious scenes, eagerly observing where other directors staged unbroken causal chains in the service of a pre-established thesis. The relationship with documentary elements, which also received expression in utilisation of comparatively cheaper original locations, also marked this first wave of films, which included Edgar Reitz's *Mahlzeiten,* Ulrich Schamoni's *Es,* Peter Schamoni's *Close Season for Foxes,* and, with reservations, Jean-Marie Straub's wilful and important adaptation of Böll's *Not Reconciled.*

A subsequent group of largely younger directors was scarcely interested in the immediate depiction of reality. The consequences of the downfall of the art of the German film also included a loss of teachers. The first group of young film-makers mainly gathered experience in shooting film shorts, and the next group learnt in the cinema itself. Klaus Lemke *(48 Stunden bis Acapulco),* Rudolf Thome *(Detektive),* and even, to start with, Fassbinder *(Liebe kälter als der Tod)* reflected in their work the action framework of the Hollywood film, and the discrepancy between cinema and reality: a dead-end since awareness was imitated at second-hand, even though it was also a possibility of making studies in the cinema. The young directors' successes with the public then began to decline though, just as with some fashionable trend. Some of them conformed, and were forgotten. The crisis intensified as did confrontations between old and young in the German film. The Film Assistance Board in West Berlin, which owed its existence to a law regulating business, stimulated a number of profitable film series, and younger directors were once again pushed to the periphery. The only clear-cut successes were provided by a number of films of works of literature, such as *Young Törless* by Volker Schlöndorff, who had learnt his trade as assistant to Melville and Malle, and Fassbinder's *Effi Briest.* They were exceptions though, in terms both of cinematic quality and of the degree of public interest attracted. These successes, coupled with the German education system's literary tradition and the lack of authors of original film scripts, have resulted up to the present day in a considerable number of German films based on works of literature. Volker Schlöndorff has celebrated his greatest successes in that sphere. His film of Böll's *The Lost Honour of Katharina Blum,* a committed and critical contribution to the discussion about anarchism, and his recent cinematic version of Grass's novel *The Tin Drum* are the positive examples of a trend towards literature which also includes many academic and uninspired adaptations such as Sinkel's *Taugenichts* or Heidi Genee's *Grete Minde.*

Younger directors, who did not feel bound to any trend, also made their way in the 1970s though. After many artistically remarkable films such as *Signs of Life* and *Land of Silence and Darkness,* Werner Herzog became an internationally recognised director with *Kaspar Hauser.* Fassbinder also took over thirty films until he was able to triumph with "The Marriage of Maria Braun" over those critics who constantly accused him of dilletantism.

One of the German cinema's problems was and certainly still is that it has not produced a genre of its own – with the minor exception of the "homeland film". Critically committed directors have nevertheless attempted to make use of the methods of this kitsch-dominated genre but these attempts – of which Reinhard Hauff's *Mathias Kneissl* was probably the most successful - soon came to a halt. The same thing happened with the West Berlin workers film aimed at a specific public. This deployed a very dry desire for sober realism in depiction of the situation facing German workers, being more directed by social theories than by experience of concrete and contradictory reality. An additional problem was posed by the fact that the documentary film is not so highly developed in the Federal Republic of Germany where Klaus Wildenhahn is the only really significant director in this sphere. He has, however, attracted a number of important pupils in the meantime, including Gisela Tuchtenhagen and other graduates of the German Academy of Film and Television in West Berlin.

The second half of the 1970s saw a reconciliation between film-makers' ambitions and the expectations of the public. That was certainly promoted by amendment of the Film Assistance Law, permitting from 1974 provision of assistance for film projects that seem likely "to improve the quality and profitability of the German film".

With *Kings of the Road* Wim Wenders made a powerfully sensitive film about two men in the German provinces; the Sinkel/Brustellin team told of the resourceful rebellion of an old lady *(Lina Braake)* with a Schweikian display of wit; Reinhard Hauff made a sceptical and cleverly popular contribution to the discussion about anarchism with his ironic *Knife in the Head;* Alexander Kluge, continuing to work without making compromises, gradually found a larger public for his uncomfortable films with *Odd jobs for a slave* and *The Patriot;* and an entire group of directors was even capable of a joint response to political reality in a film whose episodes differed considerably in quality. *Germany in Autumn,* consisting of fictional and documentary contributions, was a film without solutions and answers, and its sometimes polemical methods challenged more intensive discussion than any other German film.

The avantgarde of the German cinema – Werner Schroeter, Werner Nekes and his wife Dore O., and Rosa von Praunheim - receives international acclaim among cineastes but is known to only a limited circle in the Federal Republic and largely dependent on financial assistance from television or the Federal Ministry of the Interior.

The most important and indispensable partner for the German film is in any case television – above all by way of co-productions, which are regulated by an agreement between the film industry and the TV stations. At the same time many film producers see television as an enemy rather than just a competitor, an enemy that has alienated the public from the cinema. Such clashes, arising out of economic problems, have only been led into a more peaceful course by the fact that box office takings at cinemas have been rising again since 1978, and the number of cinemas has increased again too. That also lies behind the reconciliation between producers of "old" cinema and the younger directors.

Hans Günther Pflaum

Television

German television, the most popular mass media today, is a postwar phenomenon. A German tradition in this sphere dates back, however, to the 1880s and 1890s when Paul Nipkow developed in Berlin some of the fundamental technical preconditions for electronic transmission of moving pictures. His pioneering work earned him the name of "Father of German television". As early as 1933 Telefunken produced television sets, and during the 1936 Olympic Games at Berlin the people of the city could watch transmissions in "TV halls" – as the start of live programmes.

On July the 12th 1950, North German Radio at Hamburg transmitted the first postwar German TV picture. In November of the same year the station started the first regular TV programme, transmitted as an experiment three times a week. The official beginning of television in the Federal Republic of Germany followed on Christmas Day 1952 with the introduction of a daily evening programme lasting about two hours.

German television did not develop as a centralised institution. It developed out of the radio stations in the individual *Laender,* and from the start was linked with the organisational structure of postwar German radio. That was an outcome of the decision to decentralise Germany and to favour a federal state where the *Laender* were responsible for cultural activities. The radio was assigned culture without any long discussion, and there thus developed what is still a functioning system of regional radio stations out of which there arose the TV stations grouped in the First Programme.

The radio stations were established as public corporations so this legal form was also adopted for television. In 1961 the Federal Constitutional Court stated that: "For the organisation of radio programmes the law establishes a public institution as a legal entity, which is either free from state influence or at most subject to limited state legal supervision. Its administrative organs are de facto composed of representatives of all significant political, ideological, and social groupings in an appropriate ratio"

Mention is made there of two important characteristics basically distinguishing television in the Federal Republic of Germany from that in most other countries. German television is neither government television nor commercial television. It is largely independent of the political parties, of industry, and thus of programme policy influenced by sales strategies. At present 13 DM has to be paid monthly for use of a radio and television set in the Federal Republic.

These organisational conditions and the restriction of advertising (which is nevertheless a further source of income) to separate and short periods (a maximum of 20 minutes on workdays) before peak hours have brought German television the reputation – whether always justly so cannot be discussed here – of being one of the freest and best. This combine of regional stations established in the Association of German Radio Stations (ARD) was complemented in 1963 by Second German Television, jointly run by the *Laender* as a contrasting and alternative programme. These networks have attempted to meet wishes for minority, documentary, and educational programmes with such facilities as Schools Television, TV courses, or programmes for specific groups such as senior citizens.

Viewing figures and degrees of public interest are constantly assessed by a variety of means. The programme balance striven for between the "elitist" and the "popular" has nevertheless remained a scarcely fulfilled wish. Solution of this problem was found in establishment of regional Third Programmes. These serve an important function in providing for minorities, and have also increasingly taken on the development of new and complementary forms of education. In addition, Third Programmes have become spheres for experiment and trying out the new where fresh talents receive their first chance.

In the first years of German television, people were generally convinced that its significance extended to the electronic recording and storing of information alongside the transmission of information. All TV stations consequently equipped themselves with elaborate electronic studios (Ampex recording facilities) for the production of theatre-like television plays and light entertainment. This technology remained plausible for current affairs and for a number of specifically televisual programme forms but there was a fundamental change in the sphere of the TV play. People discovered the more flexible production procedures of the film, making it possible to do without studios.

Television thus very much contributed towards driving the country's film industry and cinemas to the brink of ruin. The bargain offered by TV as a "home cinema" led to a great reduction in cinema attendance figures. Television also transmitted many old and an increasing number of new films, thus threatening to strangle the already sick film industry here. There are, however, initial indications that this trend is beginning to be reversed as a result of a degree of weariness with television, and that attendances at cinemas are starting to mount again. Many directors, whose allegiance lay with the cinema, have been forced to adapt to television. Television became one of the largest producers of feature-film-like products in the Federal Republic of Germany, and a considerable number of younger film-makers would hardly have made their way without television. Many of them would not have been able to make a living without work for TV. It is not surprising therefore that the aesthetic characteristics of the two media have also become more similar, not always to their advantage. It thus happened not all that long ago that the people in charge of television began to make their production facilities available to the cinema. An agreement makes it possible today for films largely produced with television money to be shown in cinemas before becoming available for TV without the co-producer making any claim to a share in the cinema box-office takings. This encouragement for – and temptation towards – productions ready for risks (largely because there are no risks involved) is certainly unique.

There is hardly any German tradition of the documentary film as a popular medium. Here television has been able to provide a fresh impulse by the roundabout way of the feature and semi-documentary forms. Light entertainment also in the meantime has been almost exclusively taken over by television, which does not, however, mean that outstanding achievements in this sphere are all that frequent in the Federal Republic of Germany.

The examples presented demonstrate the possibilities open to German television. The organisation of a programme that appeals as far as possible to all paying viewers is difficult enough. The trend towards bureaucratisation is an additional obstacle there. The high degree of journalistic freedom possible as a result of the independence of TV stations in the Federal Republic of Germany undoubtedly always entails the risk of excessive one-sidedness. This freedom, however, also makes it possible to publicise and argue out conflicts that have arisen within the programme itself, which is certainly better than a controlled media system which pretends to be free of conflicts.

Discussions about private television have gained in strength again recently. They have been sparked off by publisher's involvement in the Ceefax system due to be introduced in the near future.

A resolution by the *Land* Prime Ministers (11.5.1978) provided for the implementation of four pilot projects in the sphere of cable TV, one of them supervised by the *Land* of Rhineland-Palatinate in the Ludwigshafen-Vorderpfalz area. The new agreement on North German Radio concluded in 1980 between Lower Saxony, Schleswig-Holstein, and Hamburg makes specific provision for regionalisation of the station, cable TV, and acceptance of private initiatives.

Wolfgang Längsfeld

American director Robert Aldrich during the filming of his political thriller "Twilight's Last Gleaming". This German-American co-production was made at the Bavaria Studios in Munich with Burt Lancaster as the star.

The Bavaria studios, technical facilities, and outdoor area at Geiselgasteig near Munich. "Bavaria" is one of the last big studio set-ups still at work in Europe. On the left of the photo is the reconstruction of an old Berlin street built for Ingmar Bergman's "The Serpent's Egg", and later also used by Rainer Werner Fassbinder for his film of Alfred Döblin's "Berlin Alexanderplatz".

Students from Munich's Film and Television College at work on a group production ("Fuchsmühl" 1974).

The German Academy of Film and Television (West Berlin) also provides high-level training. The photo shows Malte Ludin during the shooting of his "Kennen Sie Fernsehen?" in conclusion of his course.

Douglas Sirk, one of the grand old men of the German pre-war film and later of Hollywood, is working here on a short feature, "Bourbon Street Blues", with students from the Munich College. Rainer Werner Fassbinder (l.), who numbers Sirk among his models, acted in the production.

*The "Golden Film Ribbon", held here by actress Luise Ullrich, is, together with the
"Golden Screen", one of the most coveted film prizes in the Federal Republic. These
prizes are one element in the extensive assistance provided by the Federal and
Laender authorities. In the photo from l. to r.: Olga Tschechowa, Federal Minister of
the Interior Gerhart Baum, Luise Ullrich, Walter Giller, and Volker Schlöndorff.*

A reception given by the then Federal President Walter Scheel during the 1979 Film Festival in West Berlin. Here in conversation with the Festival director, Wolf Donner, and Sarah Maldoror, the African director.

Mario Fischl as David and Walter Taub as Rabbi Singer in Peter Lilienthal's film "David", which won the "Golden Bear" as the best film at the 1979 Berlin Festival.

A scene from Klaus Lemke's "48 hours to Acapulco".

Renata Zamengo as the Mother and Dino Melo as the Father in Werner Schroeter's poetically political film "Neapolitan siblings".

Michael Kebschull as the main character in Hark Bohm's "Moritz, lieber Moritz".

A scene from Reinhard Hauff's "Knife in the head". L. Hans-Christian Blech, r. Bruno Ganz.

Rainer Werner Fassbinder (b. 1946), one of the most prominent of German film-makers, helped re-establish the German film's international reputation. Just a few photos here from his many productions: "The Marriage of Maria Braun" with Hanna Schygulla and George Byrd (above). "Dealer of the four seasons" (above r.), and "The bitter tears of Petra von Kant" with Margrit Carstensen (l.) and Hanna Schygulla.

A scene from Werner Herzog's "Woyzeck". Klaus Kinski as Woyzeck, Wolfgang Reichmann as the Captain, and Willy Semmelrogge as the Doctor.

Volker Schlöndorff with actresses Franziska Walser (daughter of writer Martin Walser) and Angela Winkler during the filming of his contribution to "Germany in autumn".

Wim Wenders attended the Munich College and is now one of the most internationally successful younger German directors. Below: a scene from his "The American Friend" with Bruno Ganz (l.) and Dennis Hopper.

Posters for the New German Film and on behalf of the endangered cinema. Peter and Margit Sickert are among the most celebrated designers of posters and planners of advertising strategies in the Federal Republic.

Werner Herzog during the filming of his "Heart of Glass" (1976). The photo shows Herzog together with Wilhelm Friedrich who plays the foundry-owner's father.

Klaus Kinski and Isabella Adjani in Werner Herzog's "Nosferatu".

Bruno S. (r.) plays Stroszek in Werner Herzog's Film-Ballade of the same name. Centre is Clemens Scheitz and on the left Clayton Szlapinski.

Volker Schlöndorff received international acclaim for his version of Günter Grass's novel "The Tin Drum". The film won the 1979 "Golden Palm" at the Cannes International Film Festival. Above: The 12 year-old David Bennent, who plays the main character. Below: The "Tin Drum trio" during a break in filming. From l. to r.: Günter Grass, David Bennent, and Volker Schlöndorff.

A look back at films in the 1950s. Above l.: "Illusion in Moll" with Eric Pommer as director and Hildegard Knef and Hardy Krüger in the main parts. Right: director Fritz Kortner and Barbara Rütting during the filming of "Die Sendung der Lysistrata". Below: O.W. Fischer and Anouk Aimée in "Ich liebe Dich", one of the many films which Fischer also directed as well as contributing to the script.

Scientific programmes attempt to make complicated processes comprehensible even for a lay public. The photo shows a discussion, under the chairmanship of Professor Hoimar von Ditfurth (2nd from l.), in the Second Network (ZDF) programme "Querschnitt".

Reinhart Hoffmeister, Hans Magnus Enzensberger, and Karl-Heinz Bohrer (l. to r.) in the Second Network's "Litera-Tour".

"Citizens ask – Politicians answer", another Second Network (ZDF) programme. The Federal Minister of Foreign Affairs, Hans-Dietrich Genscher, faces Belgians in Brussels (below), and President Valéry Giscard d'Estaing of France answers German questions (above).

The dominance of technology. One of the longest-established programmes on German television is "What's my Line" with Robert Lembke and a guest panel. The photo shows a live transmission in a studio.

"The conspiracy", a TV film by Dieter Wedel (ZDF) with actress Andrea Jonasson.

"Oh, these ghosts" (ZDF). The photo shows Wolfgang Hinze as the credulous believer in ghosts.

Scenes from three episodes in a popular First Network (ARD) series, "Scene of the Crime". From l. to r.: Hansjörg Felmy, Herbert Stass, and Jürgen Draeger in "A shot too many"; Mady Rahl, Christoph Eichhorn, and Hans-Georg Panczak in "Bullet in the corpse"; and Hansjörg Felmy, Herbert Fleischmann, and Agnes Fink in "Decoy call".

ZDF crime series: "Derrick" with Horst Tappert (l.) in the main part of Chiefinspector Derrick, Fritz Wepper (centre), and Raimund Harmstorf; "The old man" with Siegfried Lowitz as Köster (c.), the chief character, Jan Hendriks (l.) and Alexander Golling. "The Superintendent" with Erik Ode as the main figure and his "team": Fritz Wepper, Günther Schramm and Reinhard Glemnitz (from l. to r.). Photo above.

"The suburban crocodiles", an ARD children's programme by Max von der Grün.

"Sports Studio" is a ZDF programme that attracts fans week after week.

Music programmes on the First (above) and Second (below) Networks. From l. to r.: "Record Shop" with Judy Cheeks and presenter Frank Zander; "Rock Palace" with Dickey Betts; Harald Juhnke's request programme "Music is Trumps".

"The Big Prize", a ZDF quiz programme for the benefit of physically-handicapped young people. Wim Thoelke's assistants are (from l. to r.) Janita Kühnl, Marianne Prill, Silvia Betschneider, and Beate Hopf.

The Second Network's "Hit Parade" is very popular, particularly among young people. The photo shows the programme presenter, Dieter Thomas Heck.

Joseph Beuys in "Everyone is an artist", a programme by Cologne Television (WDR).

Rainer Werner Fassbinder's film of Alfred Döblin's novel "Berlin Alexanderplatz" in 13 episodes and an epilogue was an important event on German television. The photo shows a scene from episode 9 with Günter Lamprecht and Barbara Sukowa.

"Star-Singing", an old custom during the Christmas period, telling of the journey of the Three Wise Men. Unemployed craftsmen and peacetime soldiers once used to live from the collections linked with such singing. Today the takings usually serve charitable purposes.

Customs and festivities

The problems of industrial society have also very much affected the private sphere in the Federal Republic of Germany over the past thirty years. The pressures towards the so-called affluent society have often had a negative influence on leisure hours and weekends as far as their original importance for family life is concerned. It is therefore all the more astonishing that love of traditions, pleasure in long-established festivities, and the cultivation of old customs have not been lost. Quite the contrary in fact. A renewal of interest in old traditions and a need of renewed cultivation of inter-personal relationships through sharing in celebration have become more apparent, particularly in recent years. Tradition, often said to be a legacy of the "good old days", used to regulate and determine the way people lived together and their relationships with supernatural forces. These origins still become particularly apparent, even today, in the customs associated with the time around New Year. In many parts of the country the cracking of whips, fireworks, and the noisy rollicking of masked figures are intended to stop evil spirits passing over into the New Year. Everywhere people attempt to cast a glance into the coming twelve months or to assure themselves of a little good luck for this period by making presents to one another of symbolic bringers of good fortune, or by keeping a scale from the New Year's Eve carp in their purse so as spare themselves and their families money worries.

Driving away the demons of winter and celebrating the time when days start to get longer is a very old custom. The different forms of carnival in Cologne (North Rhine-Westphalia), Mainz (Rhineland-Palatinate), and Munich (Bavaria) with their amusing masquerades and extravagant celebrations are leading examples of the wild festivities in the pre-Lent period between Twelfth Night and Ash Wednesday. A traditional meal of fish in all restaurants, inns, and pubs ends this time.

The oldest Christian festival is Easter, the day of Christ's resurrection. Easter traditions in the Federal Republic of Germany almost all derive from Germanic cultic rites in honour of Ostara, the spring goddess. From the North Sea to the Alps there have survived a large number of customs involving Easter rabbits, Easter eggs, and the healing powers of Easter water released from the ice, which all owe their origins to joy at the awakening of nature. Tradition is in general closely linked with the seasons, or rather with the significance of the seasons for man. That does not only receive expression in midsummer festivities, at their most impressive in the mountains when fires are lit on the peaks come the evening. It is also apparent during harvest festival celebrations in the autumn, in church festivities, in popular country merry-making after the exertions of the summer months, or during the bringing down of cattle from the mountains when the decorated animals return to their stalls.

One of the church festivities in Catholic areas in the Federal Republic of Germany is Corpus Christi, the Thursday after Trinity Sunday. The Church displays her splendours in festive processions in which members of the government and leading public figures participate alongside the populace. In Cologne the faithful travel in decorated boats on the Rhine, accompanied by gun salutes from the guards of honour. No-one who has seen the flower-decorated boats setting off from the Island of Women in the Corpus Christi celebration on Lake Chiem in Bavaria will ever forget that either.

The most beautiful of all German festivities, incorporating numerous customs of Christian and pagan Germanic origin, is Christmas together with the preceding time of Advent. Christ-Child or Christmas markets are held in many places from the beginning of December. In some villages and towns choirs of trombones play carols from church towers. Christmas is above all a festivity for children who have special Advent calenders for impatiently counting off the days from the 1st to the 24th of December, the day on which as darkness descends candles are lit on Christmas trees and presents exchanged in all families. New Year's Eve is celebrated with the noise of rockets and shouts of "Happy New Year". Christmas, however, is much more of a family festivity, the time of year when people are most concerned to give new life to human relationships.

Ingeborg Westermeier

Pre-Christian myths are still apparent in Alemannic carnival celebrations. Music-makers, intended to drive away spirits, at the Rose Monday procession at Schramberg (Baden-Württemberg).

Carnival in Cologne – people watching the Rose Monday procession.

Carnival, the "fifth season of the year" and the greatest German popular festivity, is not just celebrated in the main centres of Mainz, Munich, and Cologne. The photo shows "celebrants" at Bornheim near Frankfurt.

Carnival on skis on the Firstalm, Spitzingsee (Upper Bavaria).

The oldest recorded local festivity in Baden-Württemberg, the Markgröningen shepherd's race, dates back to the 15th century. 14 young shepherdesses and the same number of shepherds race barefoot across a field of stubble. Two good sheep are the tempting prizes. The photo shows the shepherdesses.

The Mülheim district of Cologne has long been associated with shipping on the Rhine. Corpus Christi is celebrated with the traditional procession of ships on the river. Thousands of people on bridges and river-banks follow the voyage of the "Cecilie" (foreground – with the sacraments) and the accompanying vessels in this "White Fleet".

Every July the small Central Franconian town of Dinkelsbühl (Bavaria) celebrates the occasion in 1632 when children saved it from being plundered by conquering Swedish troops. Over 70 members of a boys band in the rococco uniform of the Augsburg Fugger Regiment provide the music for this popular festivity.

Almost everywhere in the Federal Republic there are celebrations marking the start of summer in the night of June 21/22. The photo shows such a solstice fire on the Hochalm peak near Lenggries in Upper Bavaria.

The "1475 Landshut Wedding" is one of Europe's greatest historical presentations. During the Festival weeks every four years, the population act out the Middle Ages so as to bring to life again the resplendent marriage between Hedwig (Jadwiga), daughter of the Polish King, and Georg, son of the Duke of Bavaria. The photos show a group of children in mediaeval costumes (above), and a knightly tournament (below).

The oldest German popular festivity, dating back to the year 1035, gets under way at the statue of Roland in Bremen, a landmark for civic rights in the Middle Ages.

The Munich Beer Festival in October derives from a horse race in 1810, marking the marriage of Crown-Prince Ludwig I to Princess Therese of Sachsen-Hildburg-hausen. Today it is an attraction for millions of visitors from all over the world. The photo shows the interior of one of the festival tents with a band in traditional costume.

The North Sea and Baltic coasts with their off-shore islands and 159 landing places for fishing boats exert a particular attraction for people who live away from the sea. In many places there are celebrations at the beginning and end of the fishing season. The photo shows beflagged fishing boats with guests on board.

Decorated cows on the way to their winter quarters in the Alm in Upper Bavaria. Animals are only decorated though if they have got through the summer months without any trouble.

Among the many craft observances still preserved is the "initiation" with which the apprenticeship of book-printers and type-setters is ended. The photo shows such an initiation in Gutenberg's city of Mainz with the cathedral in the background.

Building a house has been viewed since time immemorial as a particularly important event. When the roof framework is ready, the roofing ceremony is celebrated. The joiners set a crown-like wreath or a little tree decorated with ribbons on the highest ridge. The foreman gives a speech of thanks, asks God to preserve the house and its inhabitants from misfortune, drinks to the wellbeing of the building contractor, and flings the empty glass down to the ground below. The celebrations end with a good meal.

The castle is illuminated and there are fireworks near the old bridge over the Neckar several times during the Heidelberg summer as an international attraction.

The Nuremberg Christ-Child Market. The most celebrated Christmas Market in the Federal Republic is held every year around the fountain in the square in front of the church of St. Sebaldus.

Trees at Christmas. The decorated fir tree is a symbol of the light brought into the world by the birth of Christ. It is to be found in homes and in many public places in the Federal Republic. The Midnight Mass attended by the faithful in this photo is a well-established Church tradition.

The Nikolaus celebration on December 6. This day, in remembrance of St. Nicholas, an early Christian bishop from Asia Minor, used to be linked with Germanic customs involving the driving-out of spirits. On St. Nicholas' Day nowadays, children are given sweets as part of the build-up to Christmas.

*Signing of the Fulbright Agreement in 1952 by John McCloy, the American High
Commissioner in Germany, and Federal Chancellor Konrad Adenauer. This
programme – named after its initiator, Senator J.W. Fulbright from Arkansas –
provides annually for 200 students, 50 Professors, and 20 teachers from the USA
receiving scholarships which enable them to work at German universities or schools
for a year. A similar number of German Professors, teachers, and students receive
stipendia for a year in America.*

Encounter and exchange

The information available to non-German readers of this brochure about possibilities of coming into living contact with German culture is often limited so the emphasis here will be on useful information rather than on general considerations. Attention will be confined to the most important publicly-subsidised institutions which have responsibility for provision of culture and information abroad, scholarly exchange, and development policy. These constitute the Association for International Co-operation (Vereinigung für Internationale Zusammenarbeit).

The 29th Lindau gathering of Nobel prizewinners took place in June 1979, bringing together 26 laureates from six countries and 500 scholars, students, and other visitors. The holders of scholarships from the German Academic Exchange Service (DAAD) also included students from the Chinese People's Republic for the first time. The photo shows them talking to the French prizewinner, Prof. Alfred Kastler (centre).

1. Alexander von Humboldt Stiftung (AvH)
   Jean-Paul-Strasse 12, D–5300 Bonn 2
   The Alexander von Humboldt Foundation awards research scholarships for one to two years to highly-qualified foreign scholars for carrying out work in any sphere of their own choice in the Federal Republic of Germany and West Berlin. 450 such scholarships, worth between 2,100 and 2,900 DM monthly according to scholarly qualifications, are made available every year. A separate follow-up programme is concerned with more than 7,000 former scholars, financing further scholarly work in the Federal Republic, and donating scientific equipment and specialised literature for the continuation of research in the home institute.

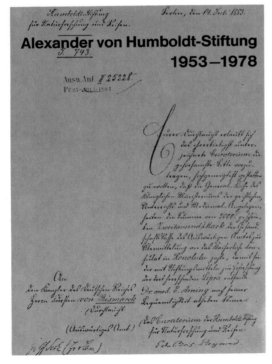

The cover of the 1978 report on the activities of the Alexander von Humboldt Foundation.

Jürgen Ziegler took part in the Carl Duisberg Society's further training programme. He is a data-processing salesman, studied at the University of Evansville for three months, and then worked for a year and a half in an American firm.

2. Carl Duisberg Gesellschaft (CDG)
Hohenstaufenring 30–32, D–5000 Köln 1
The Carl Duisberg Society disposes over 11 branches within the Federal Republic and around 100 offices in other countries. Its task is the promotion of vocational further training as part of international cultural exchange and development policy. The main emphases are provision of assistance for young Germans by way of training programmes in other industrial states, the running of similar programmes in the Federal Republic for young people from other industrial states, and the offering of individual training on behalf of UNIDO, the OECD, UNESCO, and the U.N. for specialists from both the industrialised and the developing countries. The programmes for developing countries provide further training for Third World technicians and managerial staff, and also serve the implementation of similar programmes in such specialists' home countries.

3. Deutsche Stiftung für internationale Entwicklung (DSE)
   Budapester Strasse 1, 1000 Berlin 30
   The German Foundation for International Development's main
   offices in the Federal Republic and abroad employ the following
   forms of activity for a wide variety of tasks within the sphere of co-
   operation in economic development.
   a) Seminars, conferences, and discussions between experts serving
   international and national exchanges of experience, b) different levels
   of training programme for Third World technical and managerial staff
   in a great diversity of specialised functions, and c) socio-cultural and
   technical preparatory programmes for German experts about to serve
   abroad. In addition publications, information, and other material
   about development policy and the developing countries are collected
   and made available to the general public.

*A meeting of the Club of Rome (a grouping of scientists and businessmen from
25 countries) was held at West Berlin's International Congress Centre in
October 1979 in conjunction with the German Foundation for International
Development. The theme under discussion was "The next 10 years – dangers
and opportunities". From l. to r.: Dr. Gerhard Fritz, trustee of the Foundation;
Reinhard Bühling from the German Federal Parliament and president of the
Foundation's board of trustees; Dr. Aurelio Peccei, president of the Club of
Rome; Professor Eduard Pestel, Lower Saxony Minister of Art and Science.*

4. Institut für Auslandsbeziehungen (IfA)
   Charlottenplatz 17, D–7000 Stuttgart 1
   The Institute for Foreign Relations promotes international cultural relations with all appropriate media on the basis of reciprocity. Of particular importance among the Institute's many activities are: the organisation of German exhibitions for abroad, the holding of foreign exhibitions in its "Forum for Cultural Exchange", the sending of books and magazines to other countries, the publication of books on other lands and their contemporary literature, production of a magazine on cultural exchange, the running of international symposia and seminars on Germany and other states, maintenance of the largest library specialising in other countries, the organisation of contact between regional specialists, and the provision of advisory services.

From the work of the Institute for Foreign Relations – members of the faculty of architecture at Belgrade University visiting Professor Frei Otto at the Institute for Light Structures at Stuttgart in October 1977.

5. Goethe-Institut zur Pflege der deutschen Sprache im Ausland und zur Förderung der internationalen kulturellen Zusammenarbeit e.v.
   Lenbachplatz 3, D–8000 München 2
   The Goethe Institute for Cultivation of the German Language abroad and for Promotion of International Cultural Exchange is a non-profit-making organisation. Its tasks are: the provision and promotion of the teaching of German at home and abroad; co-operation with educational administrations, institutions, and teachers in other countries; provision of specialist assistance for foreign teachers of German and Germanists; the development and improvement of teaching methods and materials; the awarding of scholarships for learning the German language and for training for foreign teachers of German; the organisation and mediation of cultural events in other countries; the provision of information abroad about cultural life in the Federal Republic of Germany; and co-operation with cultural and scholarly institutions in other countries.
   The main emphases in the work of the 175 Goethe and German Cultural Institutes in 64 countries around the world are particularly interesting: provision of German lessons; involvement in all levels of training for German teachers abroad; seminars, symposia, and lectures with scholars and journalists; readings and workshops with artists and writers; theatre tours, productions by guest directors, and festivals; musical courses and seminars; jazz and pop tours; cultural information through films, video, dias, photos, books, newspapers, tapes, and gramophone records; film shows, weeks, and festivals; film, TV, and radio seminars and workshops, sometimes with film-makers and media experts; documentary, photographic, and art exhibitions; development and running of libraries and mediatheques; and the supplying of books, language magazines, dias, tapes, films, and gramophone records.

In the language teaching room at the Murnau Goethe Institute in Upper Bavaria.

A Goethe Institute exhibition on Mies van der Rohe, the Bauhaus architect, during the "German Month" at Toulouse, France, in February 1975.

6. Deutscher Akademischer Austauschdienst (DAAD)
   Kennedyallee 50, D–5300 Bonn 2
   The German Academic Exchange Service is a self-administered organisation acting on behalf of universities in the Federal Republic of Germany and West Berlin. Its main task is to promote international relations between universities with an emphasis on academic and scholarly exchanges. The organisation has branches in London, Paris, New York, Cairo, and New Delhi, and offices in Nairobi, Rio de Janeiro, and Tokyo. An office was set up in West Berlin as early as 1964 for implementation of its activities there.

   The organisation's programmes mainly involve: scholarships for younger German and foreign scholars and students; exchanges of university teachers and study facilities for foreign scholars; university partnerships; mediation, assistance, and care for German scholars teaching at foreign universities; study trips for foreign and German groups, and also for individuals concerned with scholarship, the media, and the arts; the West Berlin artists' programme; exchanges of graduate trainees; and provision of information about the German and international university system.

   The Artist's Programme developed out of the Ford Foundation's Artists-in-Residence Programme established 15 years ago with the aim of preserving West Berlin from a threat of cultural isolation. This programme has been run since 1965 by the German Academic Exchange Service in conjunction with West Berlin's Senate, bringing an annual 20 to 25 guests for a year in the city on the Spree – artists, composers, writers, and more recently film-makers.

   The guests in West Berlin in 1980 will include such well-known authors and artists as André Glucksmann, Susan Sontag, Bernhard Luginbühl, Yannis Kounellis, Paul Armand Gette, Emmett Williams, and Franz Eggenschwiler.

7. Inter Nationes
   Kennedyallee 91–103, D–5300 Bonn 2
   Inter Nationes is a Bonn-based organisation with the task of intensifying knowledge about the Federal Republic of Germany so as to contribute towards better understanding of Germany abroad. Films, video tapes, tapes, gramophone records, books, posters, magazines, and press services are produced, assisted, or bought for distribution so as to mediate a comprehensive picture of cultural, social, economic, and political life in this country. Feature films, TV plays, and documentaries are made available for film weeks, for the work of German representatives abroad, for Cultural Institutes, and for TV stations. Books, brochures, magazines, and posters also provide information about the cultural scene in this country. An Inter Nationes translation programme assists the publication of German literature and scholarly work alongside non-fiction and books for the young in other languages. Press services in several languages are on offer for foreign newspapers and magazines. Inter Nationes also organises, on behalf of the Federal Government, information trips through the Federal Republic for foreign journalists, politicians, and representatives of the cultural professions. This visitors service has offices in Munich, Hamburg, Frankfurt/Main, and Stuttgart.

Frau Dr. Hamm-Brücher, Minister of State responsible for cultural policy abroad, at an exchange of views and information with foreign journalists.

The 1979 Kiel Week – a Polish folk-dance ensemble performing in front of the town hall.

A work by a foreign holder of a German Academic Exchange Service scholarship. George Rickey, USA – "Four open rectangles, eccentric".

The "best students of German" from 13 nations, rewarded with a trip to the Federal Republic of Germany – here in the Alte Pinakothek in Munich.

A young Spanish girl dances – to the delight of her fellow countrymen and of Germans – in the "Zeil", a celebrated shopping street in Frankfurt am Main. This photo was an entry in a photographic competition for young people entitled "Young Frankfurt".

The Peking Opera – the Chinese contribution to "Theatre of the Nations" at Hamburg in 1979.

The "Bonn Summer", an annual popular festival, presents German and foreign performers – here the Scapino Ballet from Amsterdam on the market square in summer 1978.

Henry Moore, the English sculptor, handed over his "Two Large Forms" as a loan to Federal Chancellor Helmut Schmidt in Bonn on September 19, 1979. This sculpture (left background in the photo) had been set up a few weeks previously on the rearranged forecourt to the Federal Chancellor's Office.

During the celebrations marking the 500th anniversary of the foundation of the University of Mainz, ex-premier Edward Heath gave a piano recital at the Rolandseck cultural centre.

Appendix

Supplementary addresses

Literature

Deutsche Akademie für Sprache und Dichtung, Alexandraweg 23, D–6100 Darmstadt

Gesellschaft für deutsche Sprache e.v., Taunusstraße 11, D–6200 Wiesbaden

Institut für deutsche Sprache, Friedrich-Karl-Straße 12, D–6800 Mannheim 1

Verband deutscher Schriftsteller (VS) in der Industriegewerkschaft Druck und Papier, Friedrichstraße 15, D–7000 Stuttgart 1

P.E.N.-Zentrum Bundesrepublik Deutschland, Sandstr. 10, D–6100 Darmstadt

Deutscher Autoren-Verband e.v., Sophienstraße 2, D–3000 Hannover 1

Börsenverein des Deutschen Buchhandels e.v., Großer Hirschgraben 17–21, D–6000 Frankfurt 1

Deutsche Bibliothek, Zeppelinstraße 4–8, D–6000 Frankfurt 1

Staatsbibliothek Preußischer Kulturbesitz, Potsdamer Straße 33, 1000 Berlin 30

Bibliothek des Deutschen Literaturarchivs/ Schiller-Nationalmuseum, Schiller-höhe 8, D–7142 Marbach

Bayerische Staatsbibliothek, Ludwigstraße 16, D–8000. München 22

Deutsches Literaturarchiv/ Schiller-Nationalmuseum, Schillerhöhe 8, D–7142 Marbach

Gutenberg-Museum der Stadt Mainz, Weltmuseum der Druckkunst, Lieb-frauenplatz 5, D–6500 Mainz

The visual arts

AICA: Internationaler Kunstkritikerverband, Sektion der Bundesrepublik Deutschland, Colmantstraße 15, D–5300 Bonn 1

Arbeitsgemeinschaft Bildender Künstler, Philippistraße 11, 1000 Berlin 19

Arbeitsgemeinschaft der Kunstbibliotheken, Germanisches Nationalmuseum (Bibliothek), Kornmarkt 1, D–8500 Nürnberg 11

Berliner Künstlerprogramm des Deutschen Akademischen Austauschdienstes (DAAD), Steinplatz 2, 1000 Berlin 12

Bund deutscher Landesberufsverbände Bildender Künstler, Irmgardstraße 19, D–8000 München 71

Bundesverband Bildender Künstler, Bennauerstraße 31, D–5300 Bonn 1

Bundesverband des Deutschen Kunst- und Antiquitätenhandels, Yorkstraße 11, D–3000 Hannover

Bundesverband Deutscher Galerien, Helenenstraße 2, D–5000 Köln 1

Bundesverband Deutscher Kunstversteigerer, Neumarkt 3 (Kunsthaus Lempertz) D–5000 Köln 1

Deutscher Künstlerbund Berlin (West), Kurfürstendamm 65, 1000 Berlin 15

Deutscher Kunststudenten-Verband, Am Schloßgarten 3, D–5000 Köln 41

documenta GmbH, Wolfsschlucht 2, D–3500 Kassel

Forum Bildender Künstler, Alfredistraße 2, D–4300 Essen

Gesellschaft für Bildende Kunst, Palais Walderdorff, Domfreiheit, D–5500 Trier

Gruppe RBK: Ring Bildender Künstler, Sedanstraße 68–68a (Röderhaus), D–5600 Wuppertal 2

IGBK: Internationale Gesellschaft der Bildenden Künste, Sektion der Bundesrepublik Deutschland und Berlin (West) e.V., Bennauerstraße 31, D–5300 Bonn 1

Institut für moderne Kunst, Auf der Burg 2, D–8500 Nürnberg

Internationales Kultur- und Austauschzentrum – Sektion Bildende Kunst, Berliner Straße 22, D–6000 Frankfurt

Museums and exhibitions

Deutscher Museumsbund, Senckenberganlage 25, D–6000 Frankfurt 1

ICOM: The International Council of Museums – Internationaler Museumsrat, Deutsches Nationalkomitee, Museumsinsel 1 (Deutsches Museum), D–8000 München 26

IKT: Internationale Kunstausstellungsleitertagung, Schloßstraße 1 (Berlinische Galerie), 1000 Berlin 19

Zentralinstitut für Kunstgeschichte, Meiserstraße 10, D–8000 München 2

Theatre

Deutscher Bühnenverein e.V., Bundesverband Deutscher Theater, Quatermarkt 5, D–5000 Köln 1

Genossenschaft Deutscher Bühnen-Angehöriger in der Gewerkschaft Kunst des Deutschen Gewerkschaftsbundes (GDBA), Feldbrunnenstraße 74, D–2000 Hamburg 13

Bund der Theatergemeinden e.V., Bonner Talweg 10, D–5300 Bonn 1

Dramaturgische Gesellschaft e.V., Sarrazinstraße 10, 1000 Berlin 41

Verband der deutschen Volksbühnen-Vereine e.V., Lietzenburger Straße 77, 1000 Berlin 15

Verband deutscher Freilichtbühnen e.V. – Region Nord –, Bankerheide 4, D–4700 Hamm 1

Verband deutscher Freilichtbühnen e.V. – Region Süd –, Schillerstraße 18, D–7441 Grötzingen

Verband Deutscher Bühnenverleger e.V., Bundesallee 23, 1000 Berlin 31

Deutsche Akademie der Darstellenden Künste e.V., Neue Mainzer Straße 19, D–6000 Frankfurt

Zentrum Bundesrepublik Deutschland des Internationalen Theater-Instituts e.V., Bismarckstraße 17, 1000 Berlin 12

Bund deutscher Amateurtheater, Theaterhaus am Naturtheater, D–7920 Heidenheim

Deutsche Theatertechnische Gesellschaft, Feldbrunnenstraße 74, D–2000 Hamburg

Theatersammlung der Universität Hamburg, Rothenbaumchaussee 162,
D–2000 Hamburg

Theatergeschichtliche Sammlung und Hebbel-Sammlung, Dänische Straße 15,
D–2300 Kiel

Theatermuseum München, Galeriestraße 4, D–8000 München 22

Theatermuseum Porz, Schloß, D–5050 Porz

Theatermuseum des Instituts für Theaterwissenschaft der Universität Köln,
Schloß Wahn, D–5000 Köln 90

Music

Deutscher Musikrat – Sektion Bundesrepublik Deutschland im Internationalen
Musikrat, Michaelstraße 4a, D–5300 Bonn 2

Gemeinschaft Deutscher Musikverbände, Friedrich-Wilhelm-Straße 31,
D–5300 Bonn 1

Deutscher Musikverband, Besenbinderhof 67, D–2000 Hamburg 1

Verband deutscher Musikschulen e.V., Villichgasse 17, D–5300 Bonn 2

Deutsche Orchestervereinigung e.V. im Deutschen Gewerkschaftsbund, Charlot-
te-Niese-Straße 8, D–2000 Hamburg 52

Arbeitsgemeinschaft Deutscher Chorverbände, Bernhardstraße 166,
D–5000 Köln 51

Arbeitskreis Musikpädagogischer Seminare in der Bundesrepublik Deutschland,
Briller Straße 2, D–5600 Wuppertal

Arbeitskreis für Musik in der Jugend, Deutsche Föderation Junger Chöre und
Instrumentalgruppen e.V., Fruchtallee 32, D–2000 Hamburg 19

Internationaler Arbeitskreis für Musik e.V., Heinrich-Schütz-Allee 33,
D–3500 Kassel-Wilhelmshöhe

Gesellschaft für Musikforschung e.V., Heinrich-Schütz-Allee 33, D–3500 Kassel-
Wilhelmshöhe

Institut für Neue Musik und Musikerziehung e.V., Grafenstraße 26,
D–6100 Darmstadt

Internationales Musikinstitut Darmstadt, Informationszentrum für zeitgenössische Musik, Nieder-Ramstädter-Straße 190, D–6100 Darmstadt

Deutsche Jazz-Föderation e.v., Kleine Bockenheimer Straße 12, D–6000 Frankfurt

Deutscher Komponisten-Verband, Bergengruenstraße 28, 1000 Berlin 38

Arbeitsgemeinschaft der Liedermacher AG Song, Runde-Turm-Straße 10, D–8753 Obernburg

GEMA: Gesellschaft für musikalische Aufführungs- und mechanische Vervielfältigungsrechte, Bayreuther Straße 37–38, 1000 Berlin 30

Rektorenkonferenz der Staatlichen Musikhochschulen, Dagobertstr. 38, D–5000 Köln 1

Forschungsinstitut für Musiktheater, Universität Bayreuth, D–8656 Schloß Turnau

Internationale Vereinigung der Musikbibliotheken – Deutsche Gruppe –, Salvatorplatz 1, D–8000 München 2

Musikinstrumenten-Museum des Staatlichen Instituts für Musikforschung, Bundesallee 1–12, 1000 Berlin 15

Musikinstrumentensammlung der Universität Erlangen, Schloßplatz 4, D–8520 Erlangen

Deutsches Volksliederarchiv Freiburg, Silberbachstraße 13, D–7800 Freiburg

Arts and crafts

Zentralverband des Deutschen Handwerks, Johanniterstraße 1, D–5300 Bonn 1

Zentralverband für das Juwelier-, Gold- und Silberschmiede-Handwerk, Hellstraße 18, D–4730 Ahlen

Bundesinnungsverband des Deutschen Steinmetz-, Stein- und Holzbildhauerhandwerks, Am Hirtenacker 47, D–6000 Frankfurt 90

Verband deutscher Geigenbauer Stuttgart e.V., Kernerstraße 37, D–7000 Stuttgart 1

Bundesinnungsverband für das Musikinstrumenten-Handwerk, Scheidemann-platz 2, D–3500 Kassel

Arbeitsgemeinschaft des Deutschen Kunsthandwerks e.v., Max-Joseph-Straße 4, D–8000 München 2

Gesellschaft für Goldschmiedekunst, Loogeplatz 3, D–2000 Hamburg 20

Germanisches Nationalmuseum, Kornmarkt 1, D–8500 Nürnberg

Bayerisches Nationalmuseum, Prinzregentenstraße 3, D–8000 München 22

Museum für Kunst und Gewerbe, Steintorplatz 1, D–2000 Hamburg 1

Kunstgewerbemuseum Köln, Eigelsteintorburg, D–5000 Köln 1

Gewerbemuseum Nürnberg, Gewerbemuseumsplatz 2, D–8500 Nürnberg

Die Neue Sammlung Staatliches Museum für angewandte Kunst, Prinzregenten-straße 3, D–8000 München 22

Geigenbau- und Heimatmuseum Mittenwald, Ballenhausgasse 3, D–8102 Mittenwald

Museum für Deutsche Volkskunde, Im Winkel 6/8, 1000 Berlin 33

Architecture and conservation

BDA: Bund Deutscher Architekten, Bundessekretariat, Ippendorfer Allee 14b, D–5300 Bonn 1

BDLA: Bund Deutscher Landschaftsarchitekten, e.v., Colmantstraße 32, D–5300 Bonn 1

VFA: Vereinigung Freischaffender Architekten Deutschlands e.v., Poppelsdorfer Allee 48, D–5300 Bonn 1

Bundesarchitektenkammer, Holbeinstraße 17, D–5300 Bonn 2

BDB: Bund Deutscher Baumeister, Architekten und Ingenieure e.v., Berliner Freiheit 16, D–5300 Bonn 1

Vereinigung der Landesdenkmalpfleger in der Bundesrepublik Deutschland, Schloß Biebrich, D–6200 Wiesbaden

Länderarbeitsgemeinschaft für Naturschutz, Landschaftspflege und Erholung, Calenberger Straße 2, D–3000 Hannover

Arbeitsgemeinschaft Deutscher Beauftragter für Naturschutz und Landschaftspflege e.v., Konstantin-Straße 110, D–5300 Bonn 2

Deutsche Gesellschaft für Gartenkunst und Landschaftspflege e.v., Bahnhofsplatz 8, D–7500 Karlsruhe 1

Design

Rat für Formgebung, Eugen-Bracht-Weg 6, D–6100 Darmstadt

Gestaltkreis im Bundesverband der Deutschen Industrie e.v., Oberländer Ufer 84–88, D–5000 Köln 51

Internationales Design-Zentrum Berlin e.v., Ansbacher Straße 8–14, 1000 Berlin 30

Industrieform e.v., Steeler Straße 29, D–4300 Essen 1

Institut für neue technische Form e.v., Eugen-Bracht-Weg 6, D–6100 Darmstadt

Deutscher Werkbund e.v., Alexandraweg 26, D–6100 Darmstadt

Bund deutscher Grafik-Designer e.v., Drususstraße 3, D–4000 Düsseldorf 11

Akademie für das Graphische Gewerbe, Pranckhstraße 2, D–8000 München 2

Deutsches Plakatmuseum im Museum Folkwang, Bismarckstr. 64–66, D–4300 Essen 1

AMK Berlin: Ausstellungs-Messe-Kongreß-GmbH, Messedamm 22, 1000 Berlin 19

NOWEA: Düsseldorfer Messegesellschaft mbH, Messegelände, D–4000 Düsseldorf 30

Messe- und Ausstellungs-GmbH Köln, Messeplatz, D–5000 Köln 21

Münchener Messe- und Ausstellungsgesellschaft mbH, Messegelände, D–8000 München 12

Deutsche Meisterschule für Mode, Roßmarkt 15, D–8000 München 2

Film and television

Spitzenorganisation der Filmwirtschaft e.V., Langenbeckstraße 9, D–6200 Wiesbaden

Bundesverband Deutscher Film- und AV-Produzenten e.v., Langenbeckstraße 9, D–6200 Wiesbaden

Verband der Filmverleiher e.v., Langenbeckstraße 9, D–6200 Wiesbaden

Hauptverband Deutscher Filmtheater e.v., Langenbeckstraße 9, D–6200 Wiesbaden

Verband Deutscher Spielfilmproduzenten e.v., Freystraße 4, D–8000 München 23

Arbeitsgemeinschaft Neuer Deutscher Film, Elisabethstraße 38, D–8000 München 40

Filmbewertungsstelle Wiesbaden, Schloß Biebrich, D–6200 Wiesbaden 12

Filmförderungsanstalt – Bundesanstalt des öffentlichen Rechts –, Budapester Straße 41, 1000 Berlin 30

ARD: Arbeitsgemeinschaft der öffentlich-rechtlichen Rundfunkanstalten der Bundesrepublik Deutschland, Büro, Bertramstr. 8, D–6000 Frankfurt 1

ZDF: Zweites Deutsches Fernsehen, Essenheimer Landstraße, D–6500 Mainz-Lerchenberg

German Television News GmbH, GTN-Studio am Corbusierhaus, 1000 Berlin 19

Deutscher Auslandsdienst für Rundfunk und Fernsehen, Heerstraße 58, D–5300 Bonn 2

Customs and festivities

Arbeitsgemeinschaft Deutscher Heimat-, Wander- und Naturschutzbünde, Hospitalstraße 21 B, D–7000 Stuttgart 1

Deutscher Heimatbund e.v., Friedrich-Ebert-Straße 10, D–5200 Siegburg

Deutsche Gesellschaft für Volkskunde e.v., Schloß (Ludwig-Uhland-Institut), D–7400 Tübingen 1

Verband Deutscher Heimat- und Volkstrachten-Vereine e.v., Wasserburgstraße 15, D–8013 Haar

Deutsche Gesellschaft für Freizeit e.v., Niederkasseler Straße 16, D–4000 Düsseldorf 11

Bund der Historischen Deutschen Schützenbruderschaften e.v., Hansaring 86, D–5000 Köln 1

Bund Deutscher Karneval e.v., Vereinigung zur Pflege fastnachtlicher Bräuche, Postfach 1368, D–5102 Würselen

Deutscher Schaustellerbund e.v., Sibyllenstraße 18, D–5300 Bonn 2

Deutsches Fastnachtmuseum, D–8710 Kitzingen

Encounter and exchange

Arbeitsring Ausland für kulturelle Aufgaben e.v., Oberländer Ufer 84–88, D–5000 Köln 51

AvH: Alexander von Humboldt-Stiftung, Jean-Paul-Straße 12, D–5300 Bonn 2

CDG: Carl Duisberg-Gesellschaft e.v., Hohenstaufenring 30–32, D–5000 Köln 1

DAAD: Deutscher Akademischer Austauschdienst, Kennedyallee 50, D–5300 Bonn 2

Deutsche Gesellschaft für Internationalen Jugendaustausch e.v., Lennéstraße 1, D–5300 Bonn 1

Deutsche Gesellschaft für die Vereinten Nationen e.v., Simrockstraße 23, D–5300 Bonn 1

Deutsche UNESCO-Kommission, Colmantstraße 15, D–5300 Bonn 1

Deutsches Komitee für kulturelle Zusammenarbeit in Europa e.v., Adenauerallee 214, D–5300 Bonn 1

DSE: Deutsche Stiftung für internationale Entwicklung, Endenicher Straße 41, D–5300 Bonn 1

Goethe-Institut zur Pflege der deutschen Sprache im Ausland und zur Förderung der internationalen kulturellen Zusammenarbeit e.v., Lenbachplatz 3, D-8000 München 2

Institut für Auslandsbeziehungen, Charlottenplatz 17, D–7000 Stuttgart

Institut für Internationale Begegnungen e.v., Walramstraße 9, D–5300 Bonn 2

Internationales Jugend-Kulturzentrum Bayreuth e.v., Postfach 2603, D–8580 Bayreuth

Inter Nationes, Kennedyallee 91–103, D-5300 Bonn 2

Verein für Internationale Jugendarbeit e.v., Poppelsdorfer Straße 27, D–5300 Bonn 1

Supplementary addresses

Deutsche Forschungsgemeinschaft, Kennedyallee 40, D-5300 Bonn 2

Gedok: Verband der Gemeinschaften der Künstlerinnen und Kunstfreunde, Am Karpfenteich 44, D–2000 Hamburg 63

Ständige Konferenz der Kultusminister der Länder in der Bundesrepublik Deutschland, Nassestraße 8, D-5300 Bonn 1

Verein zur Förderung von Kunst und Wissenschaft zu Bremen, Klattendick 18, D-2800 Bremen

Zentrum für Kulturforschung, Hochkreuzallee 89, D–5300 Bonn 2

Register of names

Figures in italics refer to photos or photo captions.

Adenauer, Konrad *214*
Adjani, Isabella *186*
Aicher, Otl 157
Aichinger, Ilse *26*
Aimée, Anouk *188*
Albers, Josef 36
Aldrich, Robert *178*
Almstadt, Otto *46*
Andersch, Alfred 12
Anouilh, Jean 77
Anrich-Wölfel,
  Bettina *32*
Antes, Horst 37, *42*
Armstrong, Karen *94*
Asmus, Dieter 37, *53*

Bachmann, Ingeborg 13
Baehr, Ulrich 37
Bahrs, Ulrike *129*
Bargheer, Eduard 35
Bauer, Wolfgang 77
Baum, Gerhart *50, 180*
Bausch, Pina *88*
Becker, Jürgen 13 f.
Beckett, Samuel 77
Beckmann, Max *34*
Beek, Jan Bontjes van
  115, *124*
Beethoven, Ludwig van
  97, 101, *104*
Behnisch, Günter 133,
  143
Benn, Gottfried 11 f., *18*
Bennent, David *2, 5, 187*
Berg, Alban 76
Bergengruen, Werner 11
Bergman, Ingmar *178*
Berio, Luciano 98
Bernhard, Thomas 15,
  78
Betschneider, Silvia *194*
Betts, Dickey *194*
Beuys, Joseph 37 f., *45,
  69, 196*
Bill, Max 36
Blacher, Boris 98, *107*

Blech, Hans-Christian
  183
Böhm, Gottfried 132, *145*
Böhm, Hartmut 36
Böll, Heinrich 11 f.,
  14 f., *20, 24*, 170 f.
Bohm, Hark *182*
Bohner, Gerhard 90
Bohrer, Karl-Heinz *189*
Bondy, Luc 76
Borchert, Wolfgang 11,
  19, 76
Bormann, Moritz *46*
Born, Nicolas 15
Bornemann, F. *142*
Bose, Hans-Jürgen von
  99
Boulez, Pierre 75, 98
Brahms, Johannes 97
Braun, Harald 169
Braun, Lothar 37
Brecht, Bertolt 11, 13,
  18, 77 f.
Bremer, Uwe *23*
Breuer, Leo 36
Brinkmann, Rolf Dieter
  14
Broch, Hermann 11
Brötzmann, Peter 99
Brüggemann, Antje *124*
Brüning, Peter 35
Brustellin, Alf 172
Bühling, Reinhard *218*
Busoni, Ferruccio 97
Buthe, Michael 38
Byrd, George *183*

Caduff, Sylvia *109*
Cage, John 98
Camus, Albert 12, 77
Canetti, Elias 15
Cardenal, Ernesto *11*
Carl Gustav of Swe-
  den *24*
Carossa, Hans 11
Carstensen, Margit *183*
Casals, Pablo *104*

Celan, Paul 12, *21*
Cheeks, Judy *194*
Chéreau, Patrice 75, *94*
Chotjewitz, Peter C. 15
Christina of Swe-
  den *24*
Christo *45*
Claus, Jürgen *52*
Cox, Jean *92*
Cranko, John *89*
Cuvilliés, François de *72*

Dahmen, Karl Fred 35,
  44
Dalí, Salvador 59
Dauner, Wolfgang 99
Degenhardt, Franz Josef
  13
Delius, F.C. 13
Diehl, H.J. 37
Ditfurth, Hoimar von
  189
Dix, Otto 37
Döblin, Alfred 11, *19,
  178, 197*
Doldinger, Klaus 99
Domnick, Ottomar 170
Donner, Wolf *181*
Dorn, Dieter *84*
Dorst, Tankred 77.
Draeger, Jürgen *192*
Dürer, Albrecht *53, 151*
Dürrenmatt, Friedrich
  12, 77

Eggenschwiler, Franz
  222
Eich, Günter 11, 13, *21*
Eichhorn, Christoph *192*
Eiermann, Egon 133, *138*
Einem, Gottfried von 76
Eliot, Thomas Stearns
  12, 77
Engels, Heinz *85*
Enzensberger, Hans Mag-
  nus 13 f., 170, *189*
Ernst, Max *50, 59*

Fahr, Ekkehard 133
Fassbinder, Rainer Werner 77, 169 ff., *178 f.,
183, 197*
Fehling, Jürgen 78
Feininger, Lyonel *119*
Felmy, Hansjörg *192*
Fink, Agnes *192*
Fischer, Karl von *92*
Fischer, Otto Wilhelm
188
Fischer-Dieskau, Dietrich *109*
Fischl, Mario *181*
Fleischmann, Herbert
192
Fleißer, Marieluise 78,
84
Flimm, Jürgen 76
Forsythe, William *88*
Forte, Dieter 78
Fortner, Wolfgang 98,
107
Frei, Otto *219*
Frenzel, G. 135, *152*
Frenzel, Hanna *48*
Fricker, Peter Racine 98
Fried, Erich 13, *23*
Friedrich, Caspar D. 59
Friedrich, Götz *90, 94*
Friedrich, Wilhelm *186*
Frisch, Max 12, 15, 77
Fritz, Gerhard *218*
Froboess, Cornelia *84*
Fromm, Erich 160
Fruhtrunk, Günter 36
Fry, Christopher 77
Fulbright, James William *214*
Fulda, Ludwig *19*
Furtwängler, Wilhelm
105

Ganz, Bruno *183 f.*
Gaul, Winfred 36
Geiger, Rupprecht 35
Genee, Heidi 171
Genscher, Hans-Dietrich
190
Georg (son of the
Duke of Bavaria) *206*
Gerkan-Marg, von *140*
Gerstenberg, Andreas *82*
Gerz, Jochen 38

Gette, Paul Armand 222
Giller, Walter *180*
Gilles, Werner 35
Giraudoux, Jean 77
Giscard d'Estaing, Valéry *190*
Glemnitz, Reinhard *192*
Glucksmann, André 222
Goepfert, Hermann 36
Goethe, Johann Wolfgang von 76, 78, *81, 91*
Götz, Karl Otto 35
Golling, Alexander *192*
Gorky, Maxim *82*
Grass, Günter 12 ff., *21,
25,* 169, 171, *187*
Greis, Otto 35
Grieshaber, HAP 35, *41,
162*
Gropius, Walter *119,
158*
Grosz, George 37
Grüber, Klaus Michael
76
Grün, Max von der 14,
22, 193
Gründgens, Gustaf 78 f.
Grützke, Johannes 37
Gulda, Friedrich *106*
Gutenberg, Johannes
30 f., 210

Hack, Wilhelm 57, *69*
Händel, Georg Friedrich
101
Härtling, Peter 15
Haese, Günter 36
Hagen, Nina 100
Hahmann, Friedrich *141*
Halbe, Max *19*
Hamm-Brücher, Hildegard *223*
Hampel, Gunter 99
Handke, Peter 15, 77
Harig, Ludwig 13
Harmstorf, Raimund
192
Hartmann, Karl Amadeus 98, *107*
Haubrich, Josef 57
Hauff, Reinhard 171 f.,
183
Hauser, Erich *51*
Heath, Edward *227*

Heck, Dieter Thomas
195
Hedwig (daughter
of the Polish King) *206*
Heerich, Erwin 36
Heidelbach, Karl 37
Heißenbüttel, Helmut
13 f.
Heldt, Werner 35
Hendriks, Jan *192*
Hentrich & Petschnigg
131, *139*
Henze, Hans Werner 76,
88, 98
Herzog, Werner 171,
184, 186
Hespos, Hans Joachim
98
Hesse, Hermann *18*
Heyme, Hansgünther 76
Hildesheimer, Wolfgang
13, 15, *20*
Hillebrecht, Rudolf 134
Hilpert, Heinz 78
Hindemith, Paul 76, 98
Hinze, Wolfgang *191*
Hochhuth, Rolf 13, 77
Hoehme, Gerhard 35
Höllerer, Walter *22*
Hoffmann, Peter *94*
Hoffmeister, Reinhart
189
Hollmann, Hans 76
Hopf, Beate *194*
Hopper, Dennis *184*
Horn, Rebecca 38, *47*
Horngacher, Maximilian
122
Horszowski, Mieczyslaw
104
Horvath, Ödön von 78
Huchel, Peter 11
Hüsch, Hanns Dieter 13

Ibsen, Henrik 78, *84*
Ionesco, Eugène 12, 77

Jakobi, Peter *120*
Jakobi, Ritzi *120*
Jandl, Ernst 14
Janssen, Horst 37, *41*
Jens, Walter 13, *24*
Johnson, Uwe 14, *22*
Jonasson, Andrea *191*

Jünger, Friedrich Georg 11
Jugert, Rudolf 169
Juhnke, Harald 194

Kästner, Erich 18
Käutner, Helmut 169
Kagel, Mauricio 98
Kálmán, Emmerich 76
Kampmann, Utz 36
Kandinsky, Wassily 119
Karajan, Herbert von 105
Karsunke, Yaak 13
Kaschnitz, Marie Luise 26
Kastler, Alfred 215
Kebschull, Michael 182
Keller, Rolf 11
Kellermann, Bernhard 19
Kempowski, Walter 25
Killmayer, Wilhelm 98
Kinski, Klaus 184, 186
Kipphardt, Heinar 13, 77
Kirchner, Alfred 78
Kirchner, Ernst Ludwig 34, 59
Klais, Johannes 114
Klapheck, Konrad 36
Klasen, Peter 37
Klauke, Jürgen 38
Klee, Paul 119
Klein, Yves 35
Kleist, Heinrich von 78
Klosowski, Brigitte 129
Kluge, Alexander 14, 170, 172
Knef, Hildegard 188
Knubel, Franz Rudolf 36
Koberling, Bernd 37
Koeppen, Wolfgang 15, 20
Köthe, Fritz 37
Kokoschka, Oskar 119
Kollwitz, Käthe 34
Kortner, Fritz 78, 84, 188
Kounellis, Yannis 222
Kraemer, Dieter 37
Kraemer und Sieverts 133
Kramer, Harry 36

Kreutz, Heinz 35
Krieg, Dieter 37
Kriegel, Volker 99
Kröhnke, Anka 121
Kroetz, Franz Xaver 13, 78 f., 82
Krolow, Karl 12
Krüger, Hardy 188
Küchenmeister, Rainer 37
Kühn, Beate 125
Kühn, Dieter 13, 15
Kühnl, Janita 194
Kunze, Reiner 24

Lachenmann, Helmut 98
Lamprecht, Günter 197
Lancaster, Burt 178
Lause, Hermann 81
Lausen, Jens 37
Lehár, Franz 76
Lembke, Robert 191
Lemke, Klaus 170, 182
Lenbach Franz von 245
Lenz, J.M.R. 90
Lenz, Siegfried 20
Lessing, Gotthold Ephraim 28, 76, 84
Ligeti, György 91, 98
Lilienthal, Peter 181
Lindenberg, Udo 100
Liska, Ivan 90
Liszt, Franz 97
Lodenkämper, Karolus 37
Loerke, Oskar 19
Lortzing, Albert 76
Lowitz, Siegfried 192
Ludin, Malte 179
Ludwig, Peter 57, 68
Ludwig I. (Crown-Prince) 207
Ludwig II. 92
Luginbühl, Bernhard 222
Luther, Adolf 36

Mack, Heinz 35 f.
Macke, August 34
Maderna, Bruno 98
Maldoror, Sarah 181
Malle, Louis 171
Mangelsdorff, Albert 99

Mann, Heinrich 11, 19
Mann, Thomas 11, 19
Marcks, Gerhard 119
Margarete of Denmark 24
Mattes, Eva 81
Mavignier, Almir 35
Mayer, Hans 23
McCloy, John 214
Mechtel, Angelika 26
Meistermann, Georg 35
Melo, Dino 182
Melville, Jean-Pierre 171
Menuhin, Yehudi 11
Mey, Reinhard 100
Meyer, Jobst 37
Mies van der Rohe, Ludwig 119, 132, 221
Miller, Oskar von 65
Moje-Wohlgemuth, Isgard 127
Moje, Klaus 128
Möhring, B. 154
Molo, Walter von 19
Mombert, Alfred 19
Mon, Franz 13 f.
Moore, Henry 227
Morris, William 115
Mozart, Wolfgang Amadeus 5, 76, 101
Müller-Siemens, Detlef 91, 99
Munsky, Maina-Miriam 37
Muschg, Adolf 15
Muthesius, Hermann 158

Nagel, Peter 37
Nay, Ernst Wilhelm 35
O., Dore (Nekes) 172
Nekes, Werner 172
Neuenfels, Hans 76
Neuenhausen, Siegfried 37
Neumeier, John 89
Nicholas, St. 213
Nipkow, Paul 174
Nöfer, Werner 37
Noelte, Rudolf 76, 78, 84
Nolde, Emil 34
Nono, Luigi 98
Notke, Bernt 135

O'Casey, Sean 78
Ode, Erik 192
Oelze, Richard 35
Oidtmann, H. 135
Orff, Carl 102, 107, 113
Osthaus, Karl Ernst 57

Pabst, Georg Wilhelm
169
Paetzold, Karl 122
Palitzsch, Peter 78
Panczak, Hans-Georg
192
Peccei, Aurelio 218
Pestel, Eduard 218
Petrick, Wolfgang 37
Petzold, Friederike 38
Peymann, Claus 78, 81,
91
Pfahler, Karl Georg 36
Pfitzner, Hans 98
Piene, Otto 35
Piontek, Heinz 24
Piscator, Erwin 77
Pistor, Willi 128
Pius XII. 13
Pommer, Eric 188
Praunheim, Rosa von
172
Prill, Marianne 194
Puccini, Giacomo 76

Quinte, Lothar 35

Rafeiner, Fritz 139
Rahl, Mady 192
Reichmann, Wolfgang
184
Reimann, Aribert 102
Reinshagen, Gerlind
78 f.
Reitz, Edgar 170
Reuter, Hans-Peter 37,
54
Richter, Gerhard 36, 53
Richter, Hans Werner
12, 23
Richter, Karl 109
Rickey, George 224
Rihm, Wolfgang 98
Rinke, Klaus 38
Roehr, Peter 36
Rösinger-Ohnsorge, Uta
120

Rosenbach, Ulrike 38
Rousseau, Henri 156
Rudolph, Niels-Peter 78
Rühmkorf, Peter 22
Rütting, Barbara 188
Runge, Erika 14

S., Bruno 186
Saint Phalle, Niki de 5
Sartorius, Malte 37
Sartre, Jean-Paul 12, 77
Scott, Colleen 90
Semmelrogge, Willy 184
Seuss, Juergen 165
Shakespeare, William
76, 78, 81
Shaw, George Bernard
77
Sickert, Margit 185
Sickert, Peter 185
Sinkel, Bernhard 171 f.
Siodmak, Robert 170
Sirk, Douglas 179
Sommer, Harald 77
Sonderborg, K.R.H. 35
Sontag, Susan 222
Sorge, Peter 37
Sperr, Martin 13, 78 f.
Sprengel, Bernhard 57
Süverkrüp, Dieter 13
Sukowa, Barbara 197
Sullivan, Louis 131
Sundhaußen, Helmut 36
Szlapinski, Clayton 186

Scharoun, Hans Bern-
hard 100, 132
Schamoni, Peter 170
Schamoni, Ulrich 170
Scheel, Walter 69, 181
Scheid, Karl 124
Scheid, Ursula 126
Scheitz, Clemens 186
Schiller, Friedrich 78
Schlemmer, Oskar 90,
119
Schlippenbach, Alexan-
der von 99
Schlöndorff, Volker 169,
171, 180, 184, 187
Schmalz, Josef 87
Schmidt, Arno 23
Schmidt, Helmut 227
Schnebel, Dieter 102

Schneble, Eugen 147
Schneider, Peter 15
Schnurre, Wolfdietr. 11
Schoenberg, Arnold 97 f.
Scholz, Wilhelm von 19
Schoof, Manfred 99
Schoof, Rudolf 37
Schramm, Günther 192
Schreiter, Johannes 43
Schreker, Franz 97
Schroeter, Werner 172,
182
Schüler, Ralf 144
Schüler-Witte, Ursulina
144
Schultze, Bernard 35,
43
Schulze, Freia 128
Schumacher, Emil 35,
44
Schwaiger, Brigitte 15
Schwanzer, Karl 133,
143
Schweinitz, Wolfgang
von 99, 108
Schygulla, Hanna 183

Staeck, Klaus 37, 53
Stass, Herbert 192
Stefan, Verena 15
Stehr, Barbara 124
Stehr, Hermann 19
Stein, Peter 78, 82, 84
Stockhausen, Karlheinz
98, 108
Störtenbecker, Nikolaus
37
Stoss, Veit 135, 151
Stranz, Ulrich 98
Straub, Jean-Marie 170
Strauß, Botho 15, 78
Strauß, Johann 76
Strauss, Richard 76, 98
Ströher, Karl 57, 69
Struck, Karin 15, 26
Stucken, Eduard 19

Tappert, Horst 192
Taub, Walter 181
Taut, Bruno 130
Theobaldy, Jürgen 15
Therese of Sachsen-
Hildburghausen 207

Thoelke, Wim *194*
Thome, Rudolf *170*
Trier, Hann 35
Trojahn, Manfred 98
Troll, Thaddäus *24*
Tschechowa, Olga *180*
Tuchtenhagen, Gisela *172*
Turner, William 59
Turrini, Peter 77
Tutankhamen *70*

Uecker, Günter 35, *94*
Uiberall, Bernd *46*
Uhlmann, Hans *51*
Ullrich, Dietmar 37
Ullrich, Luise *180*

Végh, Sándor *104*
Verdi, Giuseppe 76
Vesely, Herbert 170
Voth, Hannsjörg *52*
Vogel, Bernhard *69*
Volkamer, Peter 132
Vostell, Wolf 38

Waechter, Friedrich
  Karl *83*
Wagenbach, Klaus *23*
Waller, Jürgen 37
Wagner, Richard 75 f.,
  92, 94, 101
Wagner, Wieland 75, *92,
  94*
Wagner, Wolfgang 75,
  92, 94
Wallraff, Günter 14
Walser, Franziska *184*
Walser, Martin 14, *21,
  184*
Wasmuth, Johannes *155*
Webern, Anton 98
Wecker, Konstantin 100
Wedel, Dieter *191*
Weiss, Peter 13, 77
Wellershoff, Dieter 14
Wenders, Wim 172, *184*
Wendt, Ernst 78
Wepper, Fritz *192*
Wetzel, Franz 132
Weyrauch, Wolfgang 11
Wicki, Bernhard *168,*
  170

Wiechert, Ernst 11
Wildenhahn, Klaus 172
Wilder, Thornton 12
Wildgruber, Ulrich *81*
Wilding, Ludwig 36
Williams, Emmett 222
Winkler, Angelika *184*
Winkler, Bernhard 141
Wölfel, Ursula *32*
Wohmann, Gabriele *26*
Wolff, W. von *147*
Wondratschek, Wolf 15
Wunderlich, Paul *42*

Zadek, Peter 78, *81*
Zamengo, Renata *182*
Zander, Frank *194*
Ziegler, Jürgen *217*
Zimmermann, Bernd
  Alois *90,* 98
Zuckmayer, Carl *18*
  76 f., *170*
Zweig, Stefan 11

Sources of illustrations

Where there are several pictures on a page, the letters after the numbers indicate their position from r. to l. and from above to below.

Alexander von Humboldt-Stiftung, Bonn: 216; ARD/ Westdeutscher Rundfunk (WDR), Köln: 192 a–c, 193 a, 194 a+b, 196; Bettina Anrich-Wölfel, Neunkirchen: 32; Archiv Staatstheater am Gärtnerplatz, München: 164; Dorothée Antes, Karlsruhe: 42 b; ARD Pressedienst, Köln: 194 c, 197; Dieter Asmus, Hamburg: 53 a; Ausstellungs-Messe-Kongreß GmbH, Berlin (West): 144 a+b, 167 a; Alexander Baier Presse, Mainz: 49 a+d; Gert von Bassewitz, Hamburg: 90 b; Bauhaus-Archiv, Berlin (West): 119 a; Foto Bavaria, Gauting: 178 b; Bayerische Motorenwerke (BMW), München: 143 a; Bayerische Staatsoper, München: 90 a; Festspiele Bayreuth/ Siegfried Lauterwasser: 93, 95; Archiv Peter Beckmann, Ohlstadt: 34 a; Archiv Beethovenhaus, Bonn: 104; Günter Behnisch & Partner, Stuttgart: 143 b; Bildarchiv der Stadt Nürnberg: 149 a, b, 212 a; Bildarchiv der Stadt Regensburg: 148 a; Bildstelle der Stadt Bonn: 106, 147; Foto Bingel, Bad Hersfeld: 86; Börsenverein des Deutschen Buchhandels:

10; Ute Boeters, Kiel-Holtenau: 67 a–c; Boorberg Verlag, München: 27 d; Herta Borchert, Hamburg-Altona: 19 c; Braun AG, Frankfurt: 162 c; Galerie Brocksted, Hamburg: 41 c+d; Galerie Brusberg, Hannover: 42 c; Büchergilde Gutenberg, Frankfurt: 165 d; Beate Büsching, Frankfurt: 225 b; Bundesbildstelle, Bonn: 50 a, 64, 123 a+b, 148 b, 180, 181 a, 202 a+b, 214; Carl Duisberg-Gesellschaft e.V., Köln: 217; Jürgen Claus, München: 52 b; Karl Fred Dahmen, München: 44 d; Brigitte Dannehl, Köln: 112; J.H. Darchinger, Bonn 155; Archiv Deutsche Afrika-Linien, Hamburg: 139 a+b; Deutsche Bundesbahn, Frankfurt: 165 a+b; Deutsche Bundespost, Berlin (West): 7, 8, 96; Deutsche Film- und Fernsehakademie, Berlin (West): 179 c; Deutsche Presse-Agentur (dpa), Frankfurt: 24 a+b, 45 b, 81 b, 84 a–d, 85 b, 89 a, 107 a–d, 108 a+b, 109 a–c, 110, 203 b, 213, 215, 227 a; Deutscher Akademischer Austauschdienst (DAAD), Berlin (West): 222; Bildstelle Deutsches Museum, München: 65 a, 122 b; Deutsche Zentrale für Tourismus, Frankfurt: 66 a, 212 b; Foto Diedrichs-Schreiter, Neu-Isenburg: 43 c, d; Digne Meller Marcovicz, München: 26 c; Mara Eggert, Frankfurt: 83 b; Eremiten-Presse, Düsseldorf: 26 e; Filmverlag der Autoren, München: 183 c+d, 184 a, 186 a+c; Fischer Taschenbuch Verlag, Frankfurt: 22 b; Photo Fosch, München: 34 e; Michael Friedel, München: 221 a+b; Photo Friedrich, Berlin (West): 43 a; Archiv von Gerkan-Marg, Hamburg: 140; Erika Groth-Schmachtenberger, Murnau: 203 a; Hanser-Bildarchiv, München: 25 a; Carl Hanser Verlag, München: 27 e; Erich Hauser, Rottweil: 51 a; Foto Hauser, München: 44 c; H. Heidersberger, Wolfsburg: 29; Heilbronner Stimme, Heilbronn: 19 b; Hessisches Landesmuseum, Darmstadt: 69; Fritz Hiller, München: 198; Hochschule für Fernsehen und Film, München: 168, 178 a, 179 a+b, 181 b, 182 a–c, 183 a, 184 b–d, 186 b, 188 a–c; Hoffmann und Campe Verlag, Hamburg: 20 b; Elisabeth Hofmann, Hielen: 111 b; Rebecca Horn, München: 47 b, c; Maximilian Horngacher, Starnberg: 122 c; IGEDO, Düsseldorf: 166 b; Inter Nationes, Bonn: 82 b, 88, 105, 223; Institut für Auslandsbeziehungen, Stuttgart: 113 a+b, 208, 209, 210 a+b, 219; Deutsches Jagdmuseum, München: 71 a; Photo Jung, München: 41 a; Verlag Kiepenheuer & Witsch, Köln: 20 a; Klaus Kinkel, München: 42 a; Johannes Klais, Bonn: 114; Verlag Klett-Cotta, Stuttgart: 27 a+f; Kranichphoto, Berlin (West): 51 b; Kunsthalle Karlsruhe: 63 a; Verlag Kunst & Technik, München: 49 c; Landesamt für Denkmalpflege, München: 152; Landesbildstelle Berlin: 138, 142 a+b; Presseamt der Landeshauptstadt Kiel: 224; Hermann Lilienthal, Königswinter: 227 b; Limes Verlag, Wiesbaden/München: 18 b; Ingeborg Limmer, Bamberg: 151; Linke-Hoffmann-Busch, Salzgitter: 163; Luchterhand Verlag, Neuwied: 21 d, 22 c; Sammlung Ludwig, Köln: 53 c, 68a; Archiv Marburger Tapetenfabrik, Marburg: 161; Günther Meierdierks, Bremerhaven: 66 b; Klaus Meier-Ude, Frankfurt: 31 b; Wilhelm Meinberg, Ludwigshafen: 68 b; Mode-Woche-München GmbH, München: 167 b; Martina Musch, Köln: 63 c; Museum für Kunst und Gewerbe, Hamburg: 118, 119 b, 121 a+b, 124 a–e, 125, 126, 127, 128 a–c, 129 a+b; Neue Münchner Fernsehproduktion, München: 192 f; Verlag Dr. Neinhaus, Konstanz: 49 b; Fritz Neuwirth, Ottobrunn: 225 a; Uwe Niehuus, Hannover: 4; Isolde Ohlbaum, München: 25 b; Bernd Oppermann, Berlin (West): 218; Pfaff AG, Kaiserlautern: 162 b; Hermann Pfeffer, Mannheim:

33 a; Peter Peitsch, Hamburg: 226 a; Presse- und Informationsdienst, Bonn: 80 b–d; Siegfried von Quast, München 150; Regina Relang, München: 156; Hans-Peter Reuter, Karlsruhe: 54; Hans Werner Richter, München: 23 c; Uta Rösinger-Ohnsorge, Karlsruhe: 120; Frank Roland-Beeneken, Berlin (West): 83 a; Rosenthal AG, Selb: 162 a, d; Rowohlt Verlag, Reinbek bei Hamburg: 22 a, 27 b; Presse-Bild-Archiv Rainer Rüffer, Nieder-Erlenbach: 63 b; Wolfgang Rüther, Bonn: 87 b, 226 b; Ilse Ruppert, München: 48; Schaubühne am Halleschen Ufer, Berlin (West): 82 a; Bernard Schultze, Köln: 43 b; Emil Schumacher, Hagen: 44 a; Foto-Sessner, Dachau: 191 a; Peter und Margit Sickert, München: 185 a–d; Siemens AG, München: 5, 162 e; Rani A. Sifi, München: 166 a; Staatliche Landesbildstelle Hamburg: 111 a; Staatliches Hofbräuhaus, München: 207 b; Staatsbibliothek Preußischer Kulturbesitz, Berlin (West): 28; Stadtarchiv Heidelberg: 211; Stadtbücherei München: 33 b; Stadtmuseum Köln: 71 b; Stadtmuseum München: 71 c; Stadtverwaltung Mülheim: 204 a; Städtische Galerie im Lenbachhaus, München: 245 b; Klaus Staeck, Heidelberg: 53 b; Daisy Steinbeck, Datteln: 85 a; Hildegard Steinmetz, Gräfelfing: 72; Hans Stimpfl, Kiefersfelden: 87 a; Foto Studio Stuckmann, Bonn: 80 a; studiengruppe für biologie und umwelt, München: 65 b; Süddeutscher Verlag, München: 20 c, 34 c; Suhrkamp Verlag, Frankfurt: 18 a+d, 20 d, 21 a–c, 22 d; Photo Szekèkessy, Hamburg: 42 d; photo Thun, Castrop-Rauxel: 44 b; Sabine Toeffer, München: 92; Abisag Tüllmann, Frankfurt: 81 a, 91 b; Günter Uecker, Düsseldorf: 94; Ullstein Bilderdienst, Berlin (West): 19 a; Photo Umbo, Hannover: 34 e; United Artists, Frankfurt: 2, 183 b, 187 a+b; Universitätsbauamt Freiburg: 50 b; Universitätsbauamt Konstanz: 146; Verkehrsamt Baden-Baden: 165 c; Verkehrsamt Dinkelsbühl: 204 b; Verkehrsamt Köln: 70; Verkehrsamt Lenggries: 205; Verkehrsamt Neviges: 145 a; Verkehrsverein Bremen: 207 a; Verkehrsverein Landshut 206 a+b; Verlagsarchiv: 18 c, 23 b, 26 a+b, 34 b; 46 a–e, 47 a, 122 a+d, 130, 145 b, 153 a+b, 154 a+b, 245 a; Hannsjörg Voth, München: 52 a; Erika Wachsmann, Bad Homburg: 26 d; Verlag Klaus Wagenbach, Berlin (West): 23 a, 27 c; Foto Weigelt, Wuppertal: 89 b; Weltmuseum der Druckkunst, Mainz: 30, 31 a; Pressebild-Agentur Werck, Düsseldorf: 45 a; Bernhard Winkler, München: 141 a+b; Joachim Wolff, Frankfurt: 202 c; Zweites Deutsches Fernsehen (ZDF) Bildredaktion, Mainz: 91 a, 189 a+b, 190 a+b, 191 b+c, 192 d+e, 193 b, 194 d, 195; Photo Zwietasch, Kornwestheim: 41 b.

Translation: Timothy Nevill

© 1981 by Heinz Moos Verlag, Munich
In collaboration with Inter Nationes, Bonn
ISBN-3-7879-0200-7

Printing and binding: Tagblatt-Druckerei KG A. Wollenweber, Haßfurt

Printed in the Federal Republic of Germany